Prais

In *Ingaging Leadership,* Evan Hackel presents a powerful leadership philosophy that every entrepreneur needs when starting an enterprise. If you embrace his ideas and follow his advice, your people will not only work hard, but give their hearts to growing your enterprise. I recommend this book highly.

—KEVIN HARRINGTON, world-renowned entrepreneur and Original Shark on the ABC hit "Shark Tank"

As I discuss in my book *Soup,* it takes deep trust to create a truly great organization. And now in this inspiring and practical book, Evan Hackel lays out a philosophy called Ingaged Leadership that takes the concept of trust and makes it practical in so many ways."

—JON GORDON, best-selling author of *The Energy Bus* and *Soup*

Ingaging Leadership is a timely and eminently practical book that will definitely help leaders to improve their ability to bring out the best in others. The strategies and case studies Evan Hackel shares are relevant to businesses of all shapes and sizes. I particularly gained a lot from the sections on how to improve personal communication.

—GREG NATHAN, author of *Profitable Partnerships* and Founder, Franchise Relationships Institute

Ingaging Leadership

Meets the Younger Generations

Transformative concepts that will take your leadership skills to a new level, and help you build effective, productive teams and improve employee retention

EVAN HACKEL

AUTHORS PLACE
— P R E S S —

Published by Authors Place Press
9885 Wyecliff Drive, Suite 200
Highlands Ranch, CO 80126
Authorsplace.com

Copyright 2020 © by Evan Hackel
All Rights Reserved

No part of this book may be reproduced or transmitted in any form by any means: graphic, electronic, or mechanical, including photocopying, recording, taping or by any information storage or retrieval system without permission, in writing, from the authors, except for the inclusion of brief quotations in a review, article, book, or academic paper. The authors and publisher of this book and the associated materials have used their best efforts in preparing this material. The authors and publisher make no representations or warranties with respect to accuracy, applicability, fitness or completeness of the contents of this material. They disclaim any warranties expressed or implied, merchantability, or fitness for any particular purpose. The authors and publisher shall in no event be held liable for any loss or other damages, including but not limited to special, incidental, consequential, or other damages. If you have any questions or concerns, the advice of a competent professional should be sought.

All rights reserved, including the right of reproduction in whole or part in any form. For information, contact Evan Hackel, CEO, Ingage Consulting, 400 Trade Center, Suite 5900, Woburn, MA 01801. (781) 281-9390; ehackel@engage.net

Manufactured in the United States of America.

ISBN: 978-1-62865-724-1

For Paul Hackel

I believe in life finding the right mentors is one of the greatest keys to success. For me, I was extraordinarily lucky to have my father as my mentor for both my personal and my business life. What an advantage it was to be a child starting at age 10, able to work in a business with a father who was so talented and willing to teach me everything he knew. All of which was incredibly valuable, the most valuable was never what he told me, but observing how he worked and treated others. There is clearly more to leadership than what you do. How you do it makes all the difference in the world. Thank you, Dad. I love you, appreciate you, and miss you.

Table of Contents

Table of Contents

Foreword

By Howard Brodsky,
Co-Founder, Chairman and Co-Chief Executive Officer, CCA Global Partners

Over the last 25 years, I have had the privilege to work closely with Evan Hackel. When Evan joined CCA Global Partners, we were a very small company. He was our fifth employee. Evan was instrumental in helping the company grow to over 10 billion dollars in system-wide sales. Evan helped us expand and establish departments to manage Marketing, Training, National Programs, and Recruitment. He also helped us launch many new businesses, including ProSource Wholesale Floorcovering, Stone Mountain Outlet, Lender's One, Savvi Formalwear, Biking Solution and BizUnite.

Perhaps Evan's biggest accomplishment was leading our effort to turn around the Flooring America Franchise, which we bought out of bankruptcy. At that time, Flooring America was doing about $700 million in system-wide sales. Within four years with Evan as the executive in charge, Flooring America had achieved $2 billion in annual system-wide sales. Evan could never have been that successful without being the leader he is.

It has been great to watch Evan grow as a person and as leader. Early in his career, Evan wasn't the Ingaged leader he describes in this book, but over time he evolved. It has been fun and inspiring to witness the evolution of his leadership first-hand. As a leader, Evan has not taken an easy path or focused solely on the day-to-day issues of doing business. He has, in fact, committed himself to the mastery of an Ingaged Leadership approach that has required him to seek a deeper understanding of himself, the people he leads, and of the organizations where he and employees Ingage with one another to create sustainable profits and growth. I think that is remarkable.

In this compact book, Evan shares not only his philosophy of leadership, but also a range of reality-based practical solutions that support it. His advice is concise, clear, actionable, and easy-to-digest, yet powerful enough to help any leader quickly reach new levels of success.

I commend Evan for writing this book, and I recommend it highly.

What Is Ingagement and Why Do Generations Matter?

Even before you begin to read this book, you are probably wondering why I chose the title *Ingaging Leadership* rather than *Engaging Leadership*. If you visit a bookstore, you will find books about engagement. So why have I chosen to write a book about Ingagement, not engagement? What is the difference?

The first difference is that the word "Ingagement" cannot be found in dictionaries; the word "engagement" can. If you look engagement up, you will find definitions like:

- A commitment to be somewhere for a designated period of time.

- A formal agreement to get married.

- A level of belief in a process.

Of those three definitions, the third—a belief in a process—comes closest to what I mean when I refer to Ingagement. Yet Ingagement is a bigger concept; I like to say that the "I" stands for *Involvement*. Ingagement is a process where you *involve* people to make decisions. From taking part in that process, they become both engaged and Ingaged, and believe in the process.

To be clear, I'm not referring to a democratic process where people vote to make decisions. I'm talking about a process of involvement in which employees can contribute ideas so that management can make the best decisions.

A true Ingaged leader does not create phony engagement as a way to manipulate people into being involved. A true Ingaged leader genuinely believes that better ideas and processes will develop through active involvement. Ingaged leaders encourage people to support company initiatives and to contribute new ideas of their own.

That is why this book will be about *Ingagement* rather than *engagement*. Incidentally, I believe in the concept so strongly that I named my company Ingage Consulting. It is not a concept that I take lightly—I strive to live it every day.

How to Use this Book

My goal in writing this book is to present a philosophy and methodology for becoming a leader at a much higher level—an approach that I call *Ingaged Leadership*.

It has been my experience that when I discover a book that presents a lot of ideas, it is unlikely that I will use them effectively if I read it from cover to cover and then put it on a shelf. I would, therefore, like to suggest a few ways to use this book differently:

- Read the book twice – If you opt to start at the beginning and read all the way through, go back and read it for a second time. During that second reading, decide on two or three of the ideas that you would like to put into practice first.

• Use the book as a focused resource – Instead of reading the book from start to finish, use the table of contents and the index to locate the sections that can help you with your immediate needs and concerns. If you are about to revamp your approach to conducting employee reviews or hiring the best employees, for example, you can find your way quickly to the ideas you can start using immediately.

Why this Book Addresses the Issue of Managing the Younger Generations

As you have noticed, the title of this book refers to the skills needed to lead "Younger Generations." Who are the members of those generations that I will refer to throughout this book?

They are the members of the Millennial and Generation Z age groups. Let's also take a moment to discuss Baby Boomers and members of Generation X, both groups I will not include in my grouping of younger generations,

Although there are no exact, agreed-upon years that define each of these generations, they are generally defined in this way:

- Baby Boomers (who are not members of what I call the "Younger Generations") were born between about 1946 and 1964.

- Generation Xers (who are also not members of what I refer to as the "Younger Generations") were born between the mid-1960s and the early 1980s.

- Millennials were born between the mid to late 1980s and the late 1990s.

- Generation Zers were born the mid-1990s and the mid-2000s.

As you can see, these definitions overlap, are imprecise, and divisions and differences exist within them. A millennial who was born in 1985 is likely to be different from one who was born in, say, 1998. A member of Generation Z who was born in 1995 will probably have different attitudes and outlooks than one who was born in 2005.

These divisions and distinctions are not only generational, they are general. Yet as we will discover in this book, keeping them in mind can be extremely useful as you embark on the journey of leading a workforce.

CHAPTER ONE

Discovering Ingagement

Ingagement is a leadership philosophy for those who believe that it is not enough to tell people what to do, but to involve their minds, creativity and even their emotions. In this chapter, we will get a first glimpse at how Ingaged Leadership works and how powerful it can be.

W hat is the philosophy of Ingagement? It all starts with a belief that:

When you align people and create an organization where everyone works together in partnership, that organization becomes vastly more successful.

Ingagement isn't a single action that you take just once. It is an ongoing, dynamic business practice that has the power to transform your organization, your people, you, and ultimately, your success.

Everyone in a company can create Ingagement—company leaders, members of a top leadership team, middle managers and people at many organizational levels. Ingagement goes beyond the management you will find in many companies today, where top executives and middle managers believe that effective leadership means giving instructions or offering incentives.

Ingagement is different—it offers a way of moving from

good to great. Ingaged leaders trust people to participate actively in the creation and development of a strategic vision. They openly involve key stakeholders in an ongoing conversation about the organizational vision and how it can be put into action through planning and follow through.

You develop Ingaged Leadership when, through your Ingaged attitude and open listening, you let people know that you are partnering with them and that you truly listen and believe what they are saying has value.

Authenticity is key to Ingagement. When you listen sincerely, you cooperatively create plans and practices that are supported by everyone in your organization, not only initiatives that have been developed at the top.

To be clear, Ingagement doesn't mean having a democracy. In most organizations, it is the role of senior management and the board to ultimately make the best decisions for an organization in the long term. Yet when people at all levels feel heard, they are more likely to support company plans, even if their own ideas might not have been utilized completely. When people know they have been heard, they are more likely to become invested in their work; they become more eager to continue to share ideas and to cooperate. As a result, the entire organization improves and grows.

Ingagement is a highly effective way to lead members of the millennial and Generation Z groups—a cohort that I will refer to in this book as the "younger generations."

Ingaging Your Key Stakeholders

Ingagement is not limited to internal operations. When successful Ingagement extends beyond company walls, it can help you multiply your success. You can achieve such success by involving your customers, vendors, distributors, and other stakeholders in open conversation.

From a management perspective, the result is that you build an organization in which more people focus on executing the right, productive things. But getting everyone's priorities and to-do lists directed toward your organization's immediate goals is only part of the picture; both the power and the reach of Ingagement are transformative, not just habitual or "standard practice."

Let me tell you the stories of two executives I have known.

EXECUTIVE ONE

Organized, Controlling, Ineffective

I once had the opportunity to closely observe this executive because I worked in his company. For the purposes of this introduction, let's call him John.

John had a strategic vision for his company, and he was actively communicating that vision to everyone in his organization. However, John also had a non-Ingaged philosophy. He was invested in several assumptions, common in many executives.

John believed the following assumptions:

- John thought that people in his company wanted him to be someone they could "look up to." He believed it was up to him to set the company strategy, to explain the strategy to others, and to tell them what they needed to do to execute the strategy.

- John also believed that asking openly for feedback and ideas would make him a weak leader because people would believe that he lacked a cohesive, strong vision. His view was, "If I admit to people that I don't have all the answers, that I could use their help solving problems, they will doubt that I can lead them confidently."

- Leadership "style" really counted for John. He believed that if he focused closely on communicating his vision for the company with energy and conviction, he would motivate people to carry out this vision. He told me that management should be "so informed, so all-knowing, and so capable that people feel good about following."

So, how successful was John's company? It would be dishonest if I spun a tale in which the company failed utterly in the marketplace. It didn't. It is not that John's leadership style was necessarily bad. The issue is that while his leadership approach was common, it is far from optimal. I like to wonder how much more successful his organization could have become if he had practiced Ingaged Leadership because some very clear operational problems had become ingrained in John's company. Most employees were uninspired and non-supportive, and they saw problems but rarely mentioned them because they felt no one was listening.

Similar problems exist in many organizations today; new and fresh ideas do not circulate freely, and competing companies often gain an edge.

Another operational problem: John, just like the many other executives who practice his leadership philosophy, never heard from salespeople, customer service representatives, and people in other front-line positions who could have offered him a wealth of critical intelligence. Any company that falls into that pattern undermines its own competitiveness, alienates employees, and sets a ceiling on its potential for ultimate success.

EXECUTIVE TWO

An Eager but Inauthentic Listener

Let's call our second executive Paul, one who saw himself as an enlightened manager. Paul communicated often and attentively with the people in his organization.

When Paul was preparing to attend an intensive leadership workshop, he received a package of pre-workshop materials. Along with registration forms, there were worksheets to evaluate the effectiveness of Paul's leadership; one of them contained a list of questions for him to distribute to people within his organization.

One question on the worksheet asked Paul's colleagues to evaluate how well he listens. Since he had always thought of himself as a good listener, he was expecting to get positive feedback—and positive feedback was exactly what Paul got.

"People replied that I was great at listening to them," Paul recalls. "They also reported that I asked great questions and when conversations were over, they truly felt like they had been heard. Needless to say, I felt very good about the positive things that people in my organization were saying about my ability to listen."

After Paul attended the workshop, however, his upbeat feelings about his abilities as a listener changed dramatically.

"The workshop showed me that I had never been an honest and open listener," Paul now says. "In fact, I learned that I had been very manipulative; I would ask big, open-ended questions, but inside, I had a negative mindset. I was asking questions only to find out where others were wrong and where I was right. I acted like I was listening, but only to gain people's confidence so that I could uncover their weaknesses. Armed with what they told me I could prove that they were wrong."

How do I know so much about this guy named Paul? What was going on in his mind? There's a simple answer: I know those things because I am Paul. (Or maybe more accurately, because I *was* Paul.) I changed my name when writing this case study, but I am the executive who went to that workshop held at an organization called the Center for Authentic Leadership.

That workshop was the catalyst that inspired me to change the way I listen. I realized that it was time to revise an internal thought process in which I was always searching for areas where other people were wrong. Over time, I have been able to convert that process to a new one in which I am always searching for the kernel of truth in what people are saying to me. I had to transition my thought process so that I was not operating from a defensive or adversarial place, but from an inclusive one. As a result, I was able to stop being a negative leader and become one who is dedicated to positive, open, and supportive listening.

As my negative outlook and management style started to change, I discovered that I was hearing more great ideas and building on them. Of course, there were times when I did not agree completely with someone else's views, priorities, or opinions. Yet my new approach to listening and communicating created much better results, and I became a significantly more effective leader. Now members of our organizational family were able to discuss, disagree, agree, and explore new possibilities. Through that process, our organization invariably ended up with results that were far better than we had ever seen before in my organization.

I also came to realize that many executives are impostors when it comes to Ingagement, just like I was. Before I began to interact genuinely with people, I was not achieving the success I sought. Through Ingagement, the quality of ideas we all generated, including more of my ideas, increased dramatically.

From the experience of moving to an Ingaged Leadership style, I learned that people are more likely to support leaders who are willing to receive input without judgment. What a difference!

Concluding thoughts for this chapter:

The question is, how do you create Ingagement? Ingagement starts with senior management and a true belief that Ingagement will lead to a wide range of benefits including increased employee satisfaction and retention, stronger market orientation, the ability to adapt more quickly to marketplace trends and events, improved customer service and satisfaction, and higher efficiency, productivity, and profits.

So, how do you get the ball rolling? How do you start your personal and organizational progress toward success through Ingagement? We are soon to answer those questions in the chapters ahead. I invite you to turn the page, read on, and start the process now.

CHAPTER TWO

Does Ingagement Really Work?

Ingagement really works. Here is evidence that will convince you:

I f I were you, after reading the previous chapter I would be thinking, "It is great that Evan believes so strongly in Ingagement and that he feels so positive about it, but where's the proof that it actually works? Why does he feel it is so effective in managing and leading younger workers?"

Those are good questions to ask, and I have asked them about and of myself. I would like to address my answers in two ways: First, I would like to direct your attention to an appendix that you will find on page "TK" of this book. There, you will find statistics from studies that have established the effectiveness of Ingagement. In this chapter, I will offer case studies that illustrate how Ingagement has produced superlative results.

CASE STUDY ONE

Ingagement Rebuilds a Brand and Supports Profits

Let's move on to some case studies that demonstrate the effectiveness of Ingaged Leadership, the first being from my own professional life.

In the year 2000, the company I worked for, CCA Global Partners, acquired our number-one competitor, a company called Flooring America. Before our acquisition, Flooring America had 700 locations; about 400 were company-owned, and the rest were owned by franchisees.

But then the Flooring America parent company/franchisor went out of business. The circumstances were troubling, as four hundred stores that bore the "Flooring America" name had going-out-of-business sales. The brand was seriously tarnished.

The owners of those franchises were angry, frustrated, and fearful; they had to go to court to secure various concessions from their former franchisor. To make matters worse, they also had to deal with the fact that the company that had just acquired them (my company, CCA) had been their main competitor up to that point. Many of those franchisees were in no mood to even speak with people who worked at CCA. Many of them believed that we had only bought Flooring America so that we could shut down their businesses and become the dominant player in the flooring industry.

Regardless, that was not our intention. We made a commitment to bring success to the stores that had been orphaned after Flooring America's failure, and we made good on that commitment in a very big way. When we took over Flooring America, there were *270 Flooring America locations* doing *$700 million* worth of business. Only four years after we acquired Flooring America, there were close to *600 loca-*

tions that were doing *$2 billion* in business a year. In addition, the level of satisfaction among franchisees had soared—satisfaction increased to the highest level among the 15 brands that were part of CCA Global Partners.

How did we overcome resistance, rebuild a damaged brand, more than double sales, and build such high levels of satisfaction?

From day one, it was very clear to me and to my team that if we were to succeed, we would need the support and buy-in of everyone at Flooring America. So, we started a program of Ingaging everyone. In a very real sense, we needed to have a vision that would both inspire and achieve business results. If we simply tried to inspire people without an effective plan, we would fail, and if we had an effective business plan that didn't inspire people, we would fail.

We did many things to make our initiative work. We went around the country and held town hall meetings with the Flooring America owners. We wanted them to meet us and share their opinions and ideas. We addressed the most basic questions first. Did they want to retain the Flooring America name, for example, or did they think that the brand had suffered too much damage after the bankruptcy? The owners ultimately decided to keep the name.

We invited owners to rethink how the company sold floor covering. We created numerous advisory councils and did our best to encourage the owners and their staff to participate in them, and we also created an umbrella advisory council. Then, we extended the council structure and created a marketing council, a training council, a sales council, and more. By building Ingagement in those councils, we identified and created leaders within the organization.

We also started regional networking groups called "Neighborhood Networks," where individual owners got together on their own to talk about problems and share solutions that had worked for them. Were there new competitors who had opened businesses in their areas, for example? Were economic conditions in their regions improving or declining? Were there certain products that they felt could sell well to their customer base, and if so, how could those products be supported by their franchises?

Some people in CCA Global worried about what might happen if the Flooring America owners got together independently with no one from CCA there to observe or take part. But at CCA, we decided to trust the owners to meet, discuss, and develop solutions that could help everyone become more successful. Thus, we opened up lines of communication between individual owners themselves.

In cooperation with the owners and the staff, we built a five-year plan. Everyone contributed and participated in creating the plan. Through this process, a very disgruntled, upset group of individuals bonded, came together and became very passionate. The organization went from "hyper-dysfunctional" to hyper-functional.

It was a profoundly positive experience. Just to review,

we doubled the number of stores in four years and more than doubled the business.

CASE STUDY

Ingagement Works Its Magic at a Convention

The managers of a leading consumer brand approached me in 2013 with a very specific challenge. Their annual convention was coming up, an event attended by owners of their brand-specific stores across America. The executives were planning to unveil a new store design, and they wanted me to help them increase attendance at the convention.

In previous years, only about 20% of store owners had come to the convention, and it was a very big priority to get as many of them as possible to attend. Without their buy-in on the new store design, its adoption and use would not be as successful as the company leaders were hoping.

Company leaders were hoping that I could get as many as 40% or 50% of all store owners to come to the convention, but I surpassed that number. I was able to get more than 85% of storeowners there.

How did I help this company achieve those dramatic results? Plain and simple—through Ingagement. I began by asking a group of franchisees to describe their experiences at the annual conventions. Most of their comments were similar to this: "I have a lot of fun and everybody socializes, but there is no real reason for me to go. I will never learn anything that company management will not tell me via other means."

So, I went to management and asked a simple question. Instead of simply pulling the curtains off one new design at the convention, would they consider bringing three or four designs-in-progress and then allowing franchisees to make suggestions about them? Management agreed and showcased several new designs. After franchisees reviewed them, we encouraged them to make suggestions and refinements.

With the changes, I was able to shift the dynamic of the convention from "They're going to talk *to* me," to "They're going to talk *with* me." That changed the whole meeting from "95% listen and 5% contribute" to "50% listen and 50% contribute." What a difference.

The result was not only a good design, but also one that reflected the front-line, real-world intelligence that only store owners could provide. People who provided input were excited about the design that resulted because they had enjoyed a role in creating it. I predict that as stores roll out the new design, their customers are going to love it, and profits will increase.

Snapshots of Ingagement at Work

An Ingaged Leadership approach is winning acceptance in more and more businesses today. Even in organizations where the term "Ingagement" is not used, company leaders are noticing that operations simply run better when employees' contributions are heard, utilized, and rewarded. Profits grow, employee retention improves, and products are better aligned with customers' needs and desires.

Here are some short case studies of organizations where Ingagement is being used today.

- At Enterasys Networks (a division of Siemens), company leaders are achieving remarkable success from some very simple changes to increase employee Ingagement. Executives and employees at every level through the organization are encouraged to ask each other the question "What do you think?" at least once a day. Executives are also encouraged not only to implement an "open door" policy, but to remove the doors from their office entrances entirely. Vala Afshar, Chief Marketing Office and Chief Customer Officer for Enterasys Networks, writes on the SAP Business Innovation blog: "We have had incredible success with more than three years of consecutive topline revenue growth. We have also received numerous industry awards for our innovative products and services."

- At REI recreational outfitters, company leaders have created a series of "company campfire" events hosted on social media, where employees can share ideas, stories and suggestions. About 50% of all REI employees take part, which could account for the chain's strong growth in the marketplace. According to data on the company website, annual sales exceeded $2 billion in 2013, an increase of 5.9 percent from $1.9 billion the previous year.

- At **Cummins,** the maker of engines and industrial equipment, all employees are encouraged to take part side-by-side in community service projects. According to Cummins, the informal connections and interactions that take place in those settings have contributed to 2014 revenues of $19.2 billion (up from $1.65 billion in 2013) and a Fortune 500 ranking of 186 in 2013.

- When **I was working at CCA Global Partners in Manchester New Hampshire, CEO Howard Brodsky** was using a simple, yet highly effective program to build Ingagement through the ranks of his organization. Each month he held a lunch meeting for seven or eight employees, always at a local restaurant. The meetings were not exclusively for middle managers or executives; anyone could attend. "I didn't want to give the lunches a formal name," he explains, "because I wanted to keep everything somewhat loose." Yet Deb Binder, a former CCA employee who was working there at the time, recalls that "If you got an invitation to go to lunch with the CEO, that was pretty exciting." If people who had not been invited wanted to attend, they were welcome to do that. Everyone could ask anything they wanted, and no professional or personal topic was off-limits. Practical new ideas emerged from those meetings, but the greatest benefit was that people felt they were valued. Their ideas would be heard, and often tested or used, by an organization that wanted to hear what they had to say.

- When I was president at Carpet One, we took our entire staff on a retreat once a year. We did team-building exercises in the mornings, and in the afternoons, we invited all the employees to attend open meetings that were held in a big room outfitted with nothing but chairs and flipcharts. Senior management (comprised of me and the people who reported directly to me) did not attend. All the attendees were invited to walk up to a flipchart, write down any topic they pleased, and start a discussion about it. In essence, we were giving people a forum where they could discuss anything without worrying about upsetting anybody from upper management or being judged. As the meetings progressed, people were able to review the flipcharts and topics that were under discussion and offer new ideas. An extraordinary number of great ideas emerged like ideas about HR, customer service and relationships, and operational efficiency. When the retreats ended, we had people put the very best ideas on big pieces of paper from the flip charts, and when we got back to our home office, we posted those sheets on the wall, got working on them, and posted progress as it was made. People could see that their best ideas were not only heard but were put into practice. As a result, they felt motivated to suggest even more ideas—it was a real benefit to both the employees and to the organization.

- When I was at CCA, we created a series of monthly team meetings called ECHO ("Everyone Collaborates and Helps the Organization") meetings. They were unusual meetings because the participants were from three different companies that were all involved in different aspects of the floor covering business. We created subgroups by function—such as marketing, merchandising and distribution—and had meetings where members of each of those groups could meet their counterparts from the other companies. People were encouraged to discuss challenges that they were facing, to share solutions, and more. Numerous great ideas were generated, and participants discovered many new ways to cooperate, save money, and become more efficient. The participating companies realized, for example, that they could save money by using the same printer to produce their brochures. They discovered that if they shipped their displays at the same time with the same trucking company, they would save even more by negotiating lower shipping costs. Then, the ECHO participants dug a little deeper internally and found new ways to use their ideas to benefit as many different divisions of their companies as possible. All three companies benefitted because they were able to share ideas freely. They were saving money, boosting profits, generating new ideas, and building a lot of Ingagement and excitement through their ranks—it was a huge success!

- At **Carpet One**, we launched a program of 12 Town Hall meetings. First, we invited all our 780 members to contribute their ideas for our new strategic plan. We then held meetings with our Advisory Council, where those ideas were developed. Again, we hosted 12 more Town Hall meetings and presented the plan. The result was a very strong and motivational plan that we used to create an infographic that was distributed to every location, to be shared with all employees.

- **Dean Marcarelli, CCA Global Partners' Chief Marketing Officer**, used to hold off-site marketing meetings with the marketing staff of all CCA's 12 companies. People would share ideas and work on joint problems, and marketing experts were brought in to educate and stimulate new ideas for the company. From time to time Dean would invite marketing executives from companies outside of CCA to join, to add fresh perspectives to the meetings. Everyone learned, shared ideas, and cooperated. The dynamic that was created is just one more example of the transformational force of Ingaged Leadership.

Do You Have to Become an Ingaged Leader?

Can't You Practice Other Leadership Styles and Still Be Successful?

This is an important question to ask, and my honest answer is no, you are not required to master the art of Ingaged Leadership. But it is an option that is available to you, and one that I think merits your serious consideration. Consider the successes I've already shared with you—why wouldn't you want to further explore such an effective leadership strategy?"

There have been leaders in different fields—company leaders, elected officials, generals, sports coaches—who have used a top-down, directive approach instead. Some have achieved notable things, even without seeking to Ingage the hearts and minds of the people in their organizations. I am not saying those people are wrong, or that I am right. I am simply offering a different approach to leading, on what I think is a higher and more effective level of leading people— one that has worked for me, one that might work beautifully for you, and one that promises remarkable results in many of today's organizations where teamwork, personal involvement, and shared vision have brought success.

You don't have to adopt and apply every idea in this book. Nonetheless, if the philosophy of Ingaged Leadership makes sense to you, and if you find the approach worth testing, this book will help you discover new ways to achieve extraordinary things.

Concluding thoughts for this chapter:

Good things happen when you talk *with* people instead of talking *at* them. And of course, when you really listen, great things happen when you tap into the power of Ingagement.

CHAPTER THREE

Meet the Millennials and Generation Z

"Today I am managing millennial workers and I don't understand what they are
thinking or planning. Somehow, all the
rules got rewritten and I am at a loss to
know what to do."

John S., CEO

don't subscribe to the conventional wisdom that members of "younger generations" don't want to contribute to our companies and make them better. I believe that the millennial generation and Generation Z will be incredible additions to the workforce—if properly managed. Ingaging leadership is the ideal form of management for younger generations of workers,

But many businesses and their leaders are missing out on that opportunity. Consider the quote from John S. above.

I share one concern with him:

> *I worry about supervising millennial workers and the just-arriving Generation Z.*

Just to be clear, let's define our terms. The so-called millennial generation (also called "Generation Y") includes people born between 1980 and 1994. Generation Z is made up of people who were born starting in 1995. The main differences between these two generations is the impact of the

Internet. The millennium generation was born with technology. They all had computers, but they weren't born with access to the Internet—that came later. For Generation Z, the Internet was part of their lives basically from birth; access to information online is part of the picture. However, more often than millennials do, members of Generation Z use the Internet to stay in touch with their friends and peers. For example, members of Generation Z will play games with other people online, while millennials are more likely to play alone.

Although generalizations about any cohort tend to be flawed, here are some attitudes that many people my age have noticed about millennials and Generation Z:

1. **A love of technology** – If you lead a company that employs younger generations, you have noticed that they tend to access information and communicate with each other via text, Instagram, Facebook, Snapchat, Group Me and WhatsApp. New technology like Marco Polo (a video messaging tool) and Voxer (voice messaging) are just starting to become popular.

2. **An entrepreneurial mindset** – Many want to stake out a business identity and space for themselves, even in larger companies. For some leaders, this creates the impression that they are not team players in the traditional sense, though such is not the case.

3. **A love of career mobility** – Your assumption that millennials are job-hoppers could be correct. Many do

not hesitate to change jobs to achieve the personal goals and success they are looking for. In my experience, however, many millennials can be loyal and long-lasting employees, provided your organization offers them appropriate opportunities to gain recognition, "own their work," and advance.

4. Risk tolerance – Many are self-confident, happy to take risks, and willing to help their employers take chances too. That characteristic can cause misunderstanding—and even friction—with more mature leaders.

5. Social consciousness and openness – These are outlooks that all leaders would do well to embrace. Many millennials and generation Zers welcome being part of diverse workforces. Furthermore, they are more welcoming of alternative lifestyles than preceding generations were. They also tend to be compassionate and respond positively to working for companies that embrace and support social causes and "do good in the world."

ACTION STEP

Explore your attitudes about technologies. Are you accepting, curious, or do you resist learning about new things?

What's the Difference Between the Millennial Generation and Generation Z?

Realistic vs. Optimistic

Members of Generation Z are more realistic, versus the more optimistic millennial generation. The millennial generation lived through a more prosperous period of time. Generation Z on the other hand, had the experience of the great recession and saw their parents either lose their jobs or be worried about potentially losing their jobs. Such hardships made them the more pessimistic.

Generation Z expects to work harder than the millennial generation as a result of living through the great recession. This will also cause them to be more averse to risk when making career choices.

Digital Natives vs. Digital Pioneers

Millennials lived through the arrival of the technology age. They witnessed the beginnings of social media, instant messaging, search engines and smart phones. Generation Z, on the other hand, was born into it. They never knew a life other than one of interactive and interconnected community. For Generation Z, technology is not a "nice to have," it is a "need to have." For example, a Pew Research study found that 40% of Generation Z would prefer to work in an environment without a bathroom than to work without the Internet.

Private vs. Public

The millennial generation experimented with social media, loved Facebook, and shared perhaps too much of their lives. Generation Z, on the other hand, witnessed overexposure and is cautious of sharing too much information online. In fact, most of Generation Z is either not on Facebook or is on Facebook in a minimal way. They prefer Instagram and Snapchat, which offer storytelling using images rather than words.

So, Generation Z is far more partial to privacy than the millennial generation.

On-Demand Learning vs. Formal Education

The millennial generation experienced a more traditional and formal education. Generation Z, on the other hand, utilizes tools like Wikipedia, search engines, and YouTube to find out information. This has helped them develop skills of learning on-demand and will come in handy for them in the workplace. When they don't know something, they will feel comfortable discovering and learning what they need to know.

Team Players vs. Individuals

Generation Z's greater interactivity via the Internet enables them to play with friends literally from around the world, while physically at home and alone. That has made Generation Z the far greater team players when compared to the millennial generation.

Let's look at effects of the younger generations on the workforce.

Younger Generations Bring Beautiful Diversity and Varied Perspectives

Today's millennial workforce is comprised of smart young professionals who come from every part of North America, and from many other countries that are located across the globe. Taken in sum, younger generations are a wonderfully diverse group.

You could hire a consulting firm to help you decode how all members of all those groups are thinking, but if you hire younger generations, you don't have to. Their valuable perspectives are right there under the same roof with you.

Younger Generations Have Marketplace Knowledge You Need to Succeed

Whatever services or products you sell, most younger generations can provide you with the latest intelligence about what is taking place in your industry:

- What do consumers think about your products and your brand?

- How does your company compare to your competitors?

- What are the biggest trends in your industry today?

- What companies are the leaders in your sector and why?

- How do younger generations make buying decisions?

- How and when do younger generations become loyal customers?

- Do younger generations still want to purchase homes and cars, go to college, and engage in other activities that were expected among members of older generations? Or have they changed?

- What lessons can you learn and apply from cutting-edge companies like Uber, Amazon.com, and Google? Many younger generations can give you critical insights that you need.

Viewed from those perspectives, it becomes obvious your younger generation workers are one of your company's most valuable assets. Are you treating them that way?

Younger Generations Create a Culture of Learning in Your Organization

You probably think that younger generations are the "tech generation." That might be true, but even more so, they are the generation that learns. One reason for this is that many of them were in college not that long ago, and learning is ingrained in their DNA. Another is that they are part of a generation that has needed to adapt and adjust to major—and at times cataclysmic—change. Over just the last few decades, that change has included the arrival of dramatic new technologies like the Internet, new social outlooks, the changing demographics of the American population, as well as the time in office of America's first African American president.

That is a lot of change for one cohort to absorb but doing so has uniquely prepared younger generations to adapt to change. Clearly, a workforce that learns though adaptation and experience can equip any organization for success; hopefully, that success will be yours.

ACTION STEP

Step back and consider whether your organization is one that supports curiosity and learning. If not, what can you do about it?

Younger Generations Bring an Entrepreneurial Outlook to Your Company

Members of older generations generally are generally cautious, and often observe organizational hierarchies before proposing ambitious plans within their organizations. Why? Because they have been taught to do so in their professional lives. And they are generally cautious. In contrast, younger generations like to take risks, act independently, move ahead, take ownership of their work, and get things done. To unlock the benefits of those outlooks, try to lead them in these ways:

- Have the courage to let them take risks.

- Cut rules and restrictive red tape that cripple ingenuity and ambition.

- Instead of using traditional reporting relationships, create multifunctional task forces of people from different parts of your organization—teams of energetic younger generations.

- Reward younger generations, thank them, and let them move on to new challenges. In general, younger generations want to keep moving forward instead of looking back at what they have accomplished in the past.

ACTION STEP

Consider whether your organization encourages entrepreneurial thinking. If you are stifling or discouraging it, what improvements can you make?

Younger Generations Encourage Good Succession Planning

Who is going to run your company in 10, 20, or 25 years? You could hire a management consulting firm to help you create a succession plan. But if you hire, retain, and promote a superior younger workforce, you won't need to.

A thriving workforce made up of younger generation employees can act like a living, growing succession plan— possibly one that you never need to write down.

Are you welcoming younger generations to your organization and embracing all the good they bring? Or are you letting flawed misconceptions and prejudices stand in your way?

Ultimately, the decision is up to you. But if you would like your organization to succeed, I hope you will make the right choice.

ACTION STEP

Take an objective look at your succession plan. What role could your Younger Generation employees play in strengthening it?

Ingaged Leadership Is the Best Strategy for Managing and Leading Younger Generations

What is the most effective, simplest rule to follow when leading younger generations?

It is to practice the Ingaged Leadership that I explain in this book. Ingaged Leadership is a style of management that "speaks" on every level to younger generations. If you listen well, provide autonomy, encourage risk-taking and follow the other advice in this book, you will be well on your way to becoming a superior leader of millennial workers.

Here are some specific principles of Ingagement to apply:

- Practice open and Ingaged listening and communication. For younger generations, the importance of being heard is critical.

- Delay your communications. I recommend holding open meetings where employees from all ranks can present ideas in settings where company leaders are present. Capture those ideas and give younger generations the chance to take roles in putting their ideas into practice. Remember that when people—and especially younger generations—submit ideas to supervisors who stifle them, frustration builds quickly.

- Talk openly and specifically about what represents accomplishment in your organization. You should do this during job reviews, but also start earlier when you are hiring younger generations. In interviews, you can explain who you are, what you are trying to accomplish as a company, and spell out the role that applicants can play.

- Offer autonomy and opportunities for intrapreneurship. Younger generations can be good team players, yet they also expect to "make their mark" by taking ownership and achieving personal success.

- Deliver outstanding training. Training helps younger generations discover a way to grow and achieve their goals more easily in your organization.

- Engage younger generations in conversation about the future of the company. When they feel that their voices and ideas have been heard, they will become much stronger team players. They will provide more valuable insights as well.

To Summarize

Millennials are the best workers who have ever entered the workforce, and Generation Z will only be better.

Without a doubt, it takes more thought and effort to manage the younger generations. It's easier to manage people who don't question authority, don't offer innovative ideas, and who are loyal just because they feel they should be. That alone, however, does not make them great employees. In contrast, younger generation workers want to make a difference, are independent thinkers, care about the company and what it does, and are loyal when they feel it is deserved. They may be harder to manage at times, but far more productive and healthier for the organization.

Generation Z offers many of the traits of the millennials, but they are more team players, less risk-averse and more likely to look for longer-term working relationships. In my opinion, that will make them the best generation to ever enter the workplace.

Different Generations, Different Leadership Styles

I would argue that every person needs to be managed differently. Conversely, I think it could be said that every generation is attracted to different styles of leadership. The traditional top-down authoritarian leadership style was effective with the Greatest Generation and Baby Boomers, as they were very fearful of losing their jobs. As we move down the generational ladder though, more collaborative leadership styles tend to be more effective.

In developing the concepts for Ingaging Leadership, I worked to look beyond the traditional stereotypes of generations and more to the core of human needs. I wanted to inspire people by focusing on a methodology that would play to their egos and natural desire to achieve. Ingaging Leadership allows people to feel comfortable recommending changes and innovation and inspires them to accomplish more.

I have found that, with every generation I have managed, Ingaging Leadership has been an effective tool to produce superior results.

CHAPTER FOUR

Mastering the Younger Generations

With all the tools that you've learned in this book, it's time to think about them In terms of mastering your ability to lead members of the younger generations.

f you look around your organization with your eyes open and simply observe what is going on, you will be sure to notice what wonderful employees the members of younger generations are. They bring energy that radiates through your company and offer fresh new perspectives; they know what is happening in the marketplace.

To be clear, I am not suggesting that you get rid of your older employees. The institutional knowledge and expertise such employees have, generally speaking, is irreplaceable and if managed well, they can be incredibly effective members of the team.

The Big Picture

All leaders pride themselves on managing change and building legacies that will endure well into the future. I believe that one of the clearest paths to reaching those goals is to welcome, embrace, and cultivate younger generation workers who will become your organization in the years to come.

ACTION STEP

Review the principles of Ingaged Leadership explained in this book and list the strategies that will help you manage your specific group of Younger Generation employees.

Let's take a more in-depth look at some of the most effective strategies for leading younger generations.

Younger Generation Leadership Strategy One: Provide Mentors and Coaches

The ideal mentor or coach should not be a direct supervisor, but someone from another division or department—perhaps even a member of your top leadership team. Remember that the goal of coaching and mentorship is not to help your organization, but to provide support and advice to the employee who is being coached. The relationship should be all about the employee, not at all about the coach or mentor. When you establish that kind of relationship with promising members of younger generations, they understand that they are more than just workers; they are valued members of your organization.

ACTION STEP

Meet with top company executives to discuss setting up coaching and mentoring structures for Younger Generation employees.

Younger Generation Leadership Strategy Two: Create an Individual Career Plan for Each Long-Term Younger Generation Employee

When I was starting out in my career, I was comfortable with the idea that I would get promoted after "learning the ropes," making mistakes, and moving upward gradually. Most often, I would get feedback about my performance only when I went into a job review session with my boss.

In those sessions, I would get news that I was handling some aspects of my job well, and others less so. Some of my supervisors—the better ones—would outline a series of action steps and objectives for me to tackle, and then when it was time for me to have another review, I would get a little more feedback on how I was doing, and possibly some new goals to pursue.

It has been my experience that with that kind of hit-or-miss approach, giving feedback doesn't work well with younger generations for some very specific reasons. Younger generations don't like the idea of learning through trial and error; they like the sense that they are making a difference and contributing confidently to the success of your organization. Perhaps more importantly, they like to understand how they can move up and make a long-term contribution. It is best if you begin to talk about advancement and career planning with younger generation employees as soon as they arrive on the job. One good approach is to have career planning meetings with younger generations during their initial training period as new employees.

The most effective approach is to create an individual career plan for each of your younger generation employees. (Note that I am writing about employees who you can expect to remain with your organization for the long term, not temporary or seasonal employees who are in positions that will be short-lived. If you employ younger students who are only going to work for you for a short time, for example, you will not need to create individual career plans for each of them.) Here are some steps to follow:

- Ask younger generations about their personal ambitions and interests, and work with them to create a plan that lets them live out those dreams as they work for you.

- Explain the behaviors and activities that are most valued in your organization. You can say, for example, "If you can grow repeat sales in your department, we will make every effort to reward and value your contribution."

- Explain how advancement works in your company, and how it could work for your younger generation workers. If they are starting out as a salesperson in one territory, for example, they can work toward taking over a new territory after a year of hitting sales quotas and bringing in a certain number of new accounts.

- Talk about your company's values and mission and invite younger generations to tell you how they can be part of them.

- Explain management training and other development programs and lay out specifics about how younger generations can take part.

- Establish specific benchmarks and expectations for your younger generation employees to attain. Build in timelines and due dates to keep the process specific.

- Schedule future check-in meetings at regular intervals to assess how the career plan is working. Members of younger generations, like plenty of other employees, do not like to work in a vacuum. So, every month or three months, meet with them to assess how well the employee is doing with his or her career plan. At those sessions, keep the tone encouraging, and ask whether you or the company can help or provide resources.

ACTION STEP

Meet with your top executive team and representatives of your training and HR departments to plan ways to create individual development plans for as many of your employees as possible

Younger Generation Leadership Strategy Three: Replace Annual or Semi-Annual Job Reviews with Frequent Touch-Base Meetings between Younger Generation Employees and their Supervisors

Manager/employee touch-base meetings were created to be better than yearly or twice-yearly job reviews; they are especially effective when you are leading younger generations.

Why are touch-base meetings more effective than old-fashioned, standard job reviews?

First and foremost, they take place monthly, or even every few weeks, and therefore, they provide the frequent feedback that younger generations value. (Again, younger generations dislike working in a vacuum.)

What was wrong with traditional job reviews? Most are unmotivating. A supervisor usually pulls up a document that was created in the last job review and says, "Here are the to-dos we talked about last time. Have you done this? Have you done that?" Followed by the next killer question: "Well, why not?"

If you conduct reviews like these, you are sending the message that you, the manager, know everything and that your supervisee must prove him or herself. You are older, you know better, and your younger generation worker feels stifled. He or she leaves the session feeling blamed, pressured, and maybe even threatened.

There are simple, highly effective ways to turn touchbase meetings into opportunities for mentoring, coaching, and positive motivation for younger generations.

The strategy is to reverse the process so you're letting your employee take responsibility, rather than "catching" what they're doing wrong.

- **Start with a simple question.** Questions like "Has it been a good few weeks since we last talked?" or, "Have you been enjoying work lately?" kick off a give-and-take conversation that allows you to then talk about anything in a safe way. They also offer you a chance to get a general feel for how things are going for your employee.

- Replace "Let's see how you're doing on your to do list" with "What do you feel good about accomplishing since we last talked?" If you follow this advice, you will start out focusing on positive changes and accomplishments that the younger generation worker has made. Next, give positive reinforcement for what they've gotten done and let them feel proud of their achievements. Then, move on to any items that are still undone, which you can now discuss in a positive and upbeat way. This approach drains the blame from your meeting and creates positive and motivational conversations.

- Ask, "Are there areas where you need help?" This is where you can coach and assist employees. Your offer of help prevents them from feeling bad about something that is undone and lets them feel comfortable about getting the help they may need. Be sure to listen for underlying reasons why your employee might not be tackling certain tasks. The issue could be time, meaning they don't have enough of it to do everything. Perhaps others in the organization could help? It could be that they lack some piece of technology that would help them, the services of a consultant, or possibly something else. By offering assistance, you are helping someone avoid feeling guilty about not being able to get something done. Under the old system of job reviews, people would often feel shamed and want to mislead or try to divert blame from themselves—that is very unhelpful. Having a frank and honest discussion is much more effective.

- Let the employee set his or her own "to-dos" and priorities. As a supervisor, there will be times when you need to make firm assignments. But as often as you can, allow your younger generation employee to set his or her own priorities and projects, building a sense of ownership and enthusiasm.

- Observe the "five to one" rule when meeting with supervisees who could benefit from an extra dose of positive inspiration. How does it work? For every one thing you say that could be interpreted as criticism, say five things that are positive and encouraging.

After the steps I recommend above, ask your employees how they're doing on their career plan (a better name than a "to-do list") to see if anything has been overlooked. Then, ask if they have anything they would like to add to the list. You can follow up with questions like, "Why do you think this is important?" and, "How do you plan to tackle it?" If there's something you would like them to put on their list that they didn't already think of, now's the time to mention it. Most of the time, it is likely the employee has already thought of the

ACTION STEP

Augment job reviews with regular touch-base meetings for a sample group of Younger Generation workers. If they work well, plan to roll it out to include more employees.

new idea you suggest.

Younger Generation Leadership Strategy Four: Don't Let Great Younger Generation Ideas Slip through Your Fingers

An executive I know hired a young woman for his marketing department and put her to work managing some current campaigns. He found out 18 months later that she was a *bona fide* expert about marketing on social media—she practically *lived* on social media. She could have brought so much more to her new employer from day one, yet that extra value went completely untapped for a year and a half.

Call that knowledge loss, call it money wasted, or call it something worse. Whatever you call it, it's bad. How did it happen? Since I don't work for that company I can't say for sure, but it was presumably because the top executives there were all Baby Boomers. It likely never occurred to them that a new younger generation worker had ideas they needed to hear.

Is your management failing to acknowledge the contributions of younger workers? If it is, here are some steps to take to be sure you're discovering and tapping into the unique insights and skills your younger workers possess.

- **Strategy One: Uncover hidden skills during the recruiting process.** It's a mistake to screen job applicants by only saying, "Here's what you'll have to do on the job…can you cut it?" Instead, ask questions like, "We're recruiting a team to market our new app—what do you think we need to do?" Or, "We are currently using the XYZ platform to track ad usage in our franchise locations—do you know of anything better?" To use a Zen kind of paradigm, be the student, not the teacher. The things you learn could be very valuable indeed.

- **Strategy Two: Invite comments and ideas during new employee training.** Training is an ideal time to ask new hires important questions like, "How strong do you think our brand is" or, "Do our competitors do something better than we do?" If you ask questions like those, you let new employees know that you are a company that values honest and open input, and training is the place to do it. After an employee begins working for you, he or she may want to communicate big ideas only to a supervisor, where they could potentially die. Or worse, he or she might never voice those big ideas at all.

- **Strategy Three: Get some reverse mentoring going.** Reverse mentoring has become popular in many organizations. The idea of reverse mentoring is usually to have an older executive mentored about technology by a younger, tech-savvy employee. I would recommend widening that lens and having younger generations and other young workers keep your senior executives up to speed on things like marketplace trends, new products that have entered the marketplace, and news about "hot" competing companies. The wider you can cast your net for ideas from young employees, the more you benefit.

- **Strategy Four: Reward the big ideas and information that younger generations bring.** If an employee delivers a valuable piece of information to you, offer recognition, feedback, or increased responsibilities. Treat it like gold. If you don't, that bright young mind is likely to think, "Why should I tell my company anything? They ignored me the last time I did." It's up to you to offer the recognition that keeps information flowing.

Remember that younger generations have ideas, information, and skills that you need. Are you listening to them?

ACTION STEP

Meet with your divisional and departmental managers and ask them to help identify Younger Generations who have specialized knowledge that can benefit your organization.

If you aren't—let's face it—the fault lies with you. Open the doors, let the information in, and watch your company improve in ways you could never imagine.

Younger Generation Leadership Strategy Five: Invest in Training

Copious research documents the fact that younger generations like to learn. After all, they grew up attending schools and college; learning is part of the way they interact with the world.

One major study from Gallup, "How Younger Generations Want to Work and Live," reports these findings:

- 60% of younger generations say that the opportunity to learn and grow on the job is extremely important. In contrast, only 40% of Baby Boomers feel the same way.

- 50% of younger generations strongly agree that they plan to remain in their jobs for at least the next year. That might sound like a big percentage, but 60% of all other groups plan to stay in place for at least a year. Baby Boomers and others are planning on sticking around, while younger generations are weighing their options.

Findings like these document that younger generations are more likely to stay Ingaged in their jobs if they can learn.

Yet not all training takes place in a traditional classroom or corporate learning center. Here are some forms of training that appeal strongly to younger generation employees:

- **Bite-sized training on mobile devices.** I have observed that younger generations, especially, like training that is delivered to them on their phones. Even more so, they like training that is delivered in short sessions—the kind they can complete while at lunch, on break, or even at the gym.

- **Mentoring relationships with supervisors.** Gallup found that 60% of younger generations feel that the quality of the people who manage them is extremely important. With that in mind, your training for new employees can set up mentoring, not reporting, relationships between them and strategic managers. Explain how often check-ins and job reviews with their managers will happen, and what they will cover. (I am a firm believer in frequent check-ins between managers and the employees they supervise, not pro forma reviews that happen every so often.)

- **Being part of an energized and innovative team.** This is a bit of a contradiction, but at the same time, younger generations think of themselves as individualist entrepreneurs; they also expect to be part of a great team. Letting younger generations get to know their teammates during training, and fostering a sense of team/group identity, can help convince them that they have joined the right organization.

Yes, training is important to younger generations, but I encourage you to think of it as more than a chance to teach

ACTION STEP

Review your training activities and materials. Ask whether they are outdated, or new enough to appeal to your Younger Generation workers.

skills. Younger generations are the most energized, skilled, and capable generations ever to enter the workforce. Train them well and they will become your organization's brightest future.

In Summary

After reading this chapter, you might be asking why you should invest so much focused and specialized care to develop your younger generation employees. Can't you just hire them and let them do their jobs?

Of course, you could do that. But it would be short-sighted, keeping you from taking advantage of all the great things that younger generations can contribute to your organization. Any extra effort you invest in your younger workers will be repaid many times over in countless ways.

CHAPTER FIVE

Building a Strong and Ingaged Team

Effective leaders build their success by partnering with people. They take steps to recruit the right people and cultivate them after they are on board. In this chapter, we will explore effective ways to build a great team, especially one that includes members of the younger generations.

ngagement is not something that happens only at the top of your organization, or with individual managers at different levels. For Ingagement to reach its fullest potential, it should become part of your organization's DNA.

Let's take a moment to revisit "Employee Engagement: What's Your Engagement Ratio," a study conducted by the Gallup Organization that I mention in Appendix Two. To recap, research found that an increase of 70% in employee engagement yields a 240% increase in customer engagement. Companies with high levels of engagement achieve earnings per share growth at a rate that is 3.9 times greater than companies with poor employee engagement.

To quote from the study:

> *"The world's top-performing organizations understand that employee engagement is a force that drives business outcomes. Research shows that engaged employees are more productive employees. They are more profitable, more customer-focused, safer, and more likely to withstand temptations to*

leave the organization. In the best organizations, employee engagement transcends a human resources initiative—it is the way they do business."

To summarize, Ingaged employees are far more effective than non-Ingaged employees. They think and act differently, they are more collaborative, and more concerned about the success of your company. They also create a highly positive work environment.

Simply wanting Ingaged employees is not the key. The key is to cultivate Ingagement in the people who work in your organization, and to hire the *right* people. That's what this chapter is all about.

How Can You Cultivate a High Level of Ingagement?

To run a successful organization, you need to bring together a mix of people with a variety of strengths. In other words, you need variety, as embodied in a group of people who possess different strengths.

One reason to cultivate a good mix is that we all have weaknesses. Everyone in any organization has shortcomings in terms of needed skills, and it is important to recruit people who can help compensate for them.

For example, I am a person who doesn't like to get "in the weeds," meaning I don't always relish handling the day-to-day, operational side of my business, although I can handle it capably when I absolutely must. However, I bring a negative attitude to such tasks, and I tend to make mistakes—it is hardly a win-win situation. That is why I have balanced my staff by recruiting people who are incredibly detail-oriented. I can share a big idea—most often, one that the staff have helped me develop in an Ingaged way. They then can help turn that idea into a tactical plan and make it work.

So, the goal is to create a balanced staff that allows everyone to spend most of their time doing what they are good at, and what they enjoy.

The Problem with Hiring People Who Are Just Like You

Many company owners, managers, and executives make the mistake of hiring people who are just like they are or putting together teams of similarly-minded people. Software engineers tend to like to work with other software engineers, for example, and people who launched businesses by selling assertively tend to hire assertive sales professionals. As a result, their organizations fail to have the balance that they need for peak performance.

Instead, look at what's happening within your organization. As you look at your team, do you see people who are doing only what they are required to do, rather than what they love to do and at which they excel? If this is the case, your company and your team could be better served if you recruit a mix of people who together provide all the skills necessary for success.

Imagine that your business is like a symphony orchestra. Now imagine your orchestra is made up only of musicians who can play strings and tympani. What kind of music will it make? Granted, it might sound okay, but it will not make beautiful music. A full symphony orchestra usually has a group of musicians who play more than 13 different instruments, not just one or two. Chances are, your organization needs people who can perform well in a dozen or more specific roles.

ACTION STEP

Consider the variety of the people in your company. Are there gaps in ability, attitude, or experience that are preventing your organization from achieving its greatest potential? If you were starting up today, what kind of staff would allow the business to grow and prosper?

When considering your business teams, think of yourself as a conductor who, with the right mix of Ingaged people and a beautiful score, can achieve brilliant success.

Hire and Support People Who Have the Right Attitude

Attitude is the most important trait among your people.

Attitude is a game-changer. If you populate your organization with people who are positive, they will lift others and lead them to excel. On the other side of the equation, negative people can drain the energy out of everyone around them. Negative people in an organization can kill your chances of success.

I am not recommending a staff made up of people who are irrationally positive all the time like artificially upbeat cheerleaders who have no grounding in practical business. You want resilient people who adopt a strongly positive yet realistic point of view when facing business challenges and setbacks. Those will be the same people who will look for ways to make things better, even at times when everything seems to be going well.

Negativism kills. You can talk to some very skilled people who will say, "I know that everything seems to be going well right now, but I am waiting for the other shoe to drop. Negative things that are bound to happen, and things will then get worse."

Although it is good to look ahead and anticipate future problems, you want people who are going to be positive, and who are going to inspire others realistically. When people are inspired, they will perform better, and your enterprise will prosper.

Evaluate and Compare Employee Attitudes

Ron Willingham, the author of *Integrity Selling for the 21st Century* and other excellent books, has devised a very simple way to evaluate the effect of attitude on team members:

- First, evaluate the person's expertise—how much he or she knows—on a scale of 1 to 10.

- Second, evaluate his or her experience—how long he or she has been doing this kind or work—again on a scale of 1 to 10.

- Third, assess his or her attitude on a scale of 1 to 10.

- Fourth, add together the numbers from the first two steps, and multiply the result by the number from the third step.

Sample evaluations:

- Employee A rates an 8 in expertise, an 8 in experience, and a 2 in attitude. Her overall score is then 32. [(8+8) x 2 = 32]

- Employee B rates a 2 in expertise, a 4 in experience, and an 8 in attitude. His overall score is then 48. [(2+4) x 8 = 48]

Willingham's approach reveals that you can hire someone who has skills relevant to your needs and 30 years of experience, but who will still not create value for you if he or she has a negative attitude.

If you hire someone who has a can-do attitude and very little experience, he or she can have the potential to be much more productive than a negative employee with far greater experience and skill.

Make a Commitment to Invest in People

Unless you have highly motivated people who understand and are committed to your company's vision, it will be difficult for your organization to achieve its fullest potential.

If you don't already think of your people as resources to be cultivated, I urge you to start doing so by applying some or all of the practices that follow.

Create a Plan for Each Employee

The people who work for and with you are always changing; always in a state of flux. Some are improving, others are following a downward path. Some are becoming more committed to your organization, while others are growing dissatisfied. Some are developing new skills and discovering better ways of supporting your company, while others are burning out and looking for jobs elsewhere. Good companies become committed to cultivating employees. They consistently take the higher road and improve.

Employees' performance reviews offer a good setting to cooperatively create plans with them. What specific goals would employees like to reach in the coming year and beyond? What skills and experiences would *you* like them to add? If you put those expectations onto a timeline, you will have taken a good step toward helping your employees grow, become more fulfilled in their work, and become more valuable to your organization as well.

ACTION STEP

Identify several employees in your organization who would benefit if you created development plans for them. Next, write down some of the steps that you would include in that plan, such as training and spending time in other company locations. Then, try to identify more employees who could benefit if you created a plan for each of them. Finally, make some decisions about when and how you might create those plans.

Invest Wisely in Training

Training creates a company where people have superior skills, yet training can bring even larger benefits. One of the biggest is that if you invest in training, your employees will realize that they have a future with your company. That creates an environment where your best people are much more dedicated, loyal, and productive. Members of the younger generations respond positively to training.

A joke that conveys a deeper meaning:

A manager asks, "What if I invest a lot of money in training my people and then they leave me?"

Another manager retorts, "What if you don't train them and they stay?"

The reality is, it's critical to have a well-trained staff if you want better performance, but unfortunately, many companies scrimp on training.

ACTION STEP

Identify some areas in your organization where training could have the potential to improve performance dramatically. Make a plan to provide it.

Perform Regular Reviews

Reviews help ensure that the people in your organization understand your expectations and your opinions about how they are doing. Reviews are effective tools because they:

- Keep people and their work aligned with current company priorities and plans, so they are not "working blind."

- Provide important information you need to know about any current personal problems or issues that could be affecting employees' work.

- Offer a forum where you and employees can make

motivational plans for what they should achieve in the coming six months or year.

- Offer an opportunity to "take employees' temperatures" about things, like how positive they feel and how Ingaged they are.

How are you doing in this regard? If you are not conducting regular reviews, you could be causing more problems with your team members than you realize. Why? One reason is that people tend to believe the worst, not the best, if they are kept in the dark about your evaluation of them as employees.

Two Effective Ways to Conduct Reviews

- Self-evaluation prior to review – The manager and the employee each complete a review form, then meet some days later to compare and discuss their comments. In my experience, when employees evaluate themselves in preparation for a review, they do not hesitate to be critical of themselves. Although they tend to bring up areas that I wanted to raise, they often are harder on themselves than I would be.

- 360° reviews – Each employee is reviewed by not only him or herself and a supervisor, but by a group of people with whom he or she interacts on the job. My preferred way of conducting these reviews is to have people submit their evaluations of the team member who will be reviewed, then to sort the comments into categories on one master form. This process prevents the employee under evaluation from trying to guess the identity of his or her evaluators. And 360° reviews can be very effective. If an employee sees that numerous people are focusing on an area that needs improvement, those comments will be more credible than those that came from one supervisor. Alternatively, when an employee sees that people like what he or she is doing, those positive comments are more believable and encouraging.

Some insights from a sample 360° review . . .

A 360 review can communicate a wealth of information. Here are some comments I received about my own strengths and areas for potential improvement during one of my reviews:

- "As a leader, Evan is first rate. He is respectful of people and solicits opinion. He also does a good job of keeping management in the loop on high level strategic thinking and direction."

- "Evan is a strong leader with a vision. He manages different people differently according to their personality and needs. He is very responsive to staff and to members. He is very good about communicating and sharing what's going on with staff and members. He is a very hands-on manager, and he is also a very inclusive manager; one who wants to get both staff and membership more involved (e.g. many councils, monthly staff meetings)."

- "Evan is learning how to ask more questions to let others get to the right answers instead of trying to manipulate issues toward what he feels is the right path."

- "Spend more time communicating up front. This was done very well with the five-year plan, but it could be extended further. Also, I believe Evan is one of the most compassionate leaders that I have met, but this does not always come across with members and some staff members. It would be helpful if he would take the time to explain things with a little more clarity."

While that feedback isn't always pretty, it is always useful. It has been invaluable to my own interpersonal and management development. These reviews can energize your staff members too, and further the process of consistent improvement.

Two strategies to help you and your employees benefit much more from reviews ...

Let me share two strategies that I have found can dramatically improve the review process:

- Bring the company's vision into the review discussion. In reviews, I ask, "In your own words, what is the vision of the company?" I next ask, "How do you help the company achieve that vision?" Those two questions help assure that people understand the company vision, understand that it is important, and understand and recognize how they contribute.

- Give new employees a copy of the review form as soon as you hire them. This lets them know right away on what they will be reviewed. It also prevents the situation that often crops up in reviews when employees who have just gotten the form say, "I had no idea you were going to be reviewing me on these things!"

Add a plan to take reviews one step further:

Reviews are more than scorecards; they provide an opportunity to build a plan with each employee. What are the key areas the employee should focus on in the next year, for example? What is he or she doing well that can be built upon? What areas of improvement can they work on over the next 12 months? Once you've agreed together on goals, set check-in points and incorporate them in a training and development plan. Regardless of the type of review you choose, the process can produce motivating action plans for

ACTION STEP

Assess the way your organization conducts reviews. Consider regularity, approach, methodology, and look for areas ripe for improvements.

learning and growth.

Remember that Benefits Matter

Offering excellent benefits to the people in your company is expensive—no question—but it is critical to cultivating and retaining a strong employee base. As we noted at the start of this chapter, your staff is your greatest asset.

Benefits keep people within your organization. If you are not providing comprehensive healthcare coverage and another company offers a better package, people in your company will seek positions at that other company. The same is true in relation to funding a 401(k)—millennials and members of Generation Z are looking for good benefits in the companies where they accept jobs.

Investing in benefits ultimately means that you will retain your best employees and reduce turnover, which is expensive. To find a replacement for an employee who leaves is expensive and often a waste of time. You have to spend money and time to recruit each new employee, usually while the job of the employee who left is being handled by other staffers or is left undone. After you bring your new employee on board, it costs money for the training that gets him or her up to speed. And in some cases, the first person you hire doesn't work out. He or she fails to serve customers well while getting up to speed, for example, which costs you money and business. And if that new hire doesn't work out, you have to repeat the entire process a second or even a third time.

Those steps are hugely expensive. Yet in many cases, you can prevent them by simply having an excellent benefits plan.

I have been a small businessperson and I have worked for large companies. I am fully aware of how time-consuming and expensive it is for small businesses to offer good benefits.

ACTION STEP

Review your benefits plan by comparing it to those that are being offered by other companies where your employees could be looking for jobs. If your benefits aren't in the ballpark, you could be encouraging your people to leave you.

But the reality is that doing so is worth it; the money you invest is money well spent.

Look for Value Fit

Even the most skilled and hardworking employees might not be the best people for your organization, particularly if their values do not fit with those of your company. If your company's values include a commitment to listening to customers and exceeding their needs, for example, a manager who doesn't like to listen to customers might not be the best person to have on your staff, even if he or she seems to be meeting the requirements of the job.

When an employee is a solid performer, but does not fit the corporate values, you face a difficult challenge. Unfortunately, such employees are unlikely to change just because you tell them to "be more collaborative," or "spend more time being an active listener." You can, however, provide educational training or other opportunities for them to learn to be more collaborative or improve their communication skills.

Some value problems might be insurmountable. Dishonesty and a lack of integrity, for instance, are causes for termination.

It might be a controversial idea, but when people reach a certain age (maybe age 30), it can be more difficult for them to change the way they think. They have grown up learning a certain set of values, and changing those values is challenging for them and for you as an executive.

Strategies for Recruiting and Hiring Ingaged Staff Members

This book is not meant to be a handbook on hiring; there are many excellent books out there that are. However, I would like to offer some suggestions on hiring the right people, from my perspective, that can help you cultivate a more Ingaged organization.

To evaluate listening:

Chances are that you will not gain much insight into a job candidate's listening skills by asking, "Are you a good listener?" But you *can* learn a lot by paying attention to how well people actively listen during interviews. When you ask open-ended questions, do they listen well enough to respond directly to the questions you ask, as well as any subtext?

To evaluate openness:

Ingagement is the central theme of this book, yet in interviews, it can be difficult to evaluate a job candidate's desire to communicate in the open and committed way that supports Ingagement.

You could say something like, "In our company, we value openness. Do you value openness?" Yet because the person you are interviewing would like to be hired, chances are the he or she will reply, "Oh yes, I value it very much." (Candidates are unlikely to say, "I know it is a core value of your company, but I don't value it.")

The following questions can help you assess how open the potential employee has been in the past, and how much value he or she places on openness:

- "Tell me about a time when a colleague or manager couldn't deal with opinions that differed from his or hers. What did you do?"

- "In what areas in our company do you think openness would be effective? Where would it be ineffective?"

- "What are some examples from your career that demonstrate that you value openness?"

- "Can you tell me about a work situation when someone's openness and honesty had been beneficial?"

These are probing and effective questions, and it is difficult for candidates to lie on the spot or misrepresent themselves while answering them.

Question to evaluate other key areas:

- To evaluate orientation toward results – "Tell me about a time when you completed a task that demonstrated your focus on results."

- To evaluate honesty – "Share an example of a time when someone acted dishonestly. What did you do, what were the results, and can you tell me what your take-away lesson was?"

- To evaluate the desire to collaborate – "Have you ever collaborated with other people to solve a problem? What did you learn that you believe you could apply to working here?"

When you ask people to reflect on past experiences with such questions, you elicit deeper information about what they believe and practice. You also have an improved ability to understand how well they will fit in your organization.

Concluding thoughts for this chapter:

Many employees will respond to the strategies that I explain in this book and become fully Ingaged in your organization. While I hesitate to end this chapter on a negative note, I would like to observe that there are times when letting the wrong people go sooner rather than later is the wisest decision you can make.

If someone does not share company values (or does not care to do so), if he or she has shown dishonesty, if he or she is autocratic and uninterested in Ingaging with other members of your team, letting that person go can be a wise decision indeed.

ACTION STEP

I recently attended an excellent presentation by Jeremy McKinley, a very smart man who is a member of the top marketing team at Trek Bicycle. He was discussing his strategies for marketing and brand success. One of his slides said simply, "Fire Someone – You Know Who It Is." Although his slide caused people to laugh, it became somewhat clear in the discussion that followed that most of the people in the room believed in what it said – and believed that they could benefit from letting certain people go.

CHAPTER SIX

Practical Ways to Master the Art of Ingaged Management

Ingagement, like any practical leadership philosophy, needs to be put into practice every day in a variety of situations and contexts. To do that, you need a toolbox of skills that you can apply when necessary.

The Ingaged organization you will build can be like a beautiful, fast, and responsive automobile. It is one where members of all groups and generations contribute freely. It will be capable of taking you anywhere, quickly. But because you will be the driver at the controls, you have some decisions to make: How and where will you steer the car? Who will give *you* directions? When should you speed up and when should you slow down? When will your beautiful automobile need repairs, a rebuild, or just a simple tune-up so that it can continue to operate smoothly and efficiently?

I know that is just an analogy, and analogies tend to be flawed. Nevertheless, let's explore some practical concepts that can help you lead your organization to the right destinations and achieve exceptional results.

Define and Address the Causes of Problems, Not the Symptoms

If you are trying to solve a problem in your organization, here is an important question to ask:

Are you addressing the symptoms of the problem, or the cause?

Let's say, for example, that your salespeople are not meeting your expectations or sales quotas. In many organizations, leaders will define the problem in just that way, saying, "Our salespeople are bad at selling, that's the problem."

However, if those company leaders dug deeper, they could identify root causes of the problem that, if addressed, could lead to more effective solutions. The root problems could be issues like:

- We do not have the best products to compete in the marketplace.

- We do not have the right pricing.

- We have supply or delivery problems that cause our customers to buy from our competitors.

- Our customer service is not good enough to motivate first-time buyers to become repeat customers.

- We have a training or coaching problem.

- We are not taking steps to be sure that we hire the right salespeople.

- We are not equipping our salespeople with the right tools.

ACTION STEP

Think of an issue that you are facing in your company – a problem that you are trying to solve. Try to dig deeper and deeper down until you have identified all the possible root causes of it. Then decide which of them to address first, and how. Remember that other people will be able to offer you a wider range perspectives and suggestions than you can generate if you attempt to define or solve the problem on your own.

To pinpoint the root cause of the problem, you can ask questions like:

- "Why do you think we have a sales problem?"

- "What are our most successful salespeople doing to sell this product?"

- "What are those successful salespeople *not* doing?"

- "Are there any marketing issues related to this problem?"

- "Are we applying the same effective selling approaches that our competitors use?"

Again, you need to keep digging down to find the root of the cause. You also need to talk to all the people involved—people from the sales team, the marketing team, and other appropriate personnel—to get at the underlying issues. Be sure to talk with customers and potential customers too.

Tap the Power of Collaboration

Leaders at many companies typically use the term "collaboration" to describe brainstorming sessions that are held to generate ideas around a specific topic or problem. The leaders of those companies often seem to believe that effective collaboration means getting people together into the same room to air big ideas.

I see the power of collaboration as being so much more; it goes beyond generating ideas and gives people a sense of ownership. When people genuinely collaborate, they become invested in the success of current processes and the overall success of your organization.

Even if you are extremely astute in business and know what needs to be done to succeed, I encourage you to still involve your team in finding solutions.

If you go to your team and say, "Here are the answers to our current challenge, and this is what I want us to do," their initial reaction will be to evaluate what they're being told—it's just human nature. They will ask themselves questions like, "Do I like his idea? How does it impact me? Is it really a good idea? Isn't there a better answer or solution?"

You will discover that you can achieve far better results if you bring people together and say, "We need to work together on this issue. I have some ideas, and I'm sure you have ideas, too. What do we need to do?" If you spend time thinking about it and discussing it as a group, and if you are open to letting people make improvements to your best ideas, the end result will be a group of people working together to make the best solutions happen.

So, collaboration isn't just about making better ideas. It's about building Ingagement and effectiveness to make *great* things happen.

CASE STUDY

There are demonstrable benefits of collaboration, yet nonetheless, many executives don't take the time to collaborate. Instead, they fall back into the traditional management style of, "If I ask people to do something, they should just do it."

My family's business was a classic example. We had a salesperson who was phenomenal; he typically outsold all the other salespeople in the company. When he would request simple and basic favors from the people he worked with, such as things he needed for his customers, he was typically met with resistance. He got such a reaction because he didn't take time to tell people *why* he needed what he was requesting. He didn't ask for opinions—he wouldn't collaborate at all. As a result, the other employees became resentful and weren't eager to do what he asked, but he couldn't understand why. When I explained why he encountered such resistance (and by now all you readers should understand that it had something to do with his lack of Ingagement), his response was, "Well, I'm the top salesperson so if I just say to do it, that should be good enough."

His authoritarian attitude started to negatively affect his business. At a certain point he realized in order to continue selling successfully, he needed to adjust.

He started taking the time to involve the other employees by saying, "I have an issue with a client. Here is what is going on," and "I need some help—do you have any suggestions? Have you tried something that has worked better?" The other members of the team became supportive, and if they had a better idea, they had an opportunity to share it.

In time, he grew and ended up closing 10 times more sales than the average salesperson did. Through Ingagement, he built success through the support of his company team and his customer team as well.

Remember That "Because I said so" is Not Good Enough

If you are a company leader or a manager who supervises a staff, the reality is that "Just because I asked" isn't good enough. In the short term you can bully or intimidate people, but for the durable health and success of your organization, you need to take steps like these toward fuller collaboration:

- **Explain** why you want something done.

- **Ask** people for their opinions.

- **Strive** to approach challenges in better and alternative ways.

You should not take these steps because they make people feel better, but because they lead to better outcomes.

ACTION STEP

Reflect on how you talk to people and request their ideas and help. Do you take the time to explain the issue you are facing? Do you check to ensure that they understand why you are asking? Do you leave an opening for them to suggest better ideas and solutions?

Get in the Habit of Asking for Help

Very few people like to ask for help—it's a personality thing. Some people are just too shy to ask. Others hesitate to ask because they feel they are bothering or inconveniencing other people. Further, some feel that if they ask for help, they will appear incapable, unintelligent, or unresourceful.

I have a totally different take on this issue based on my experience. I am convinced other people feel validated and appreciated when I ask them for help. I also believe that people typically enjoy giving help because we all naturally feel good about helping others. Another benefit is that when someone helps you, they sense that you "owe" them a favor in return. That can establish a pattern of healthy cooperation and give-and-take.

I often say to people, "Please ask me for help if you ever need anything." Even if I don't say that, people know they can come to me because I have established a pattern of being helpful. Such efforts have helped build deeper relationships and greater organizational success.

I'm not suggesting you ask for help just for the sake of asking for help, or just to make people feel good. When you do need help, however, don't shy away from asking—people will appreciate you more. When you ask people for assistance, you demonstrate that you respect their expertise and effort, which will then help create a stronger bond between you and those around you.

An added benefit? Asking for help tells others that you know you're not perfect. It shows a more human side to you as a leader. It's not a weakness, it's a strength; you show that you are strong enough to know you need to ask for help. Asking for help is a sign that you're a confident person, not an arrogant one.

ACTION STEP

Over the next few days, consciously take time to ask people for more help. Consider their reactions. Over time, evaluate how your relationships with those people have improved.

Focus on Key Performance Indicators

There is so much power in the simple process of identifying and monitoring performance indicators. When you do, you become involved in what your employees focus on and what they need to achieve. When they achieve the levels of improvement you have set as goals, your people will have the ability to congratulate themselves on success.

Ultimately, when you do those things, the bottom line that you care about—your net profits—will improve as a result. Profit is not a Key Performance Indicator; it is a result. Key Performance Indicators are measures of the activities that will improve your profitability if you handle them well. They could be as simple as the number of new customers you acquire in every quarter or every year, your inventory levels, or your in-stock levels.

Sample Key Performance Indicators

Here are some performance indicators that you might decide to monitor:

- Average sale size
- Customer satisfaction rates or Net Promoter Score
- Days from order to delivery
- Employee Ingagement levels
- The closing rates of sales
- The cost of goods sold
- The number of new sales leads that you are generating
- The number of sales per employee
- Website traffic

Take Time to Frame How You See Things

I love to ski, but I really love skiing through groves of trees. The trick to successfully skiing in the trees is not to look at the trees, but at the path between them.

The same is true about business—it is best to think about what you need to *do* to be successful, not what you need to avoid.

If you think about what you need to avoid while skiing—i.e. the trees—you are far more likely to hit the trees. People are naturally drawn to what they think about. For better outcomes, focus your attention instead on what needs to be done to be successful, not on problems to avoid.

Often, it's as simple as saying things differently:

- Ask, "Where can we find new areas to operate with greater efficiency?" instead of "We need to cut costs."

- Or ask, "What do we need to learn about our customers' most pressing concerns?" rather than, "We can't lose any more customers."

Framing things positively can have a huge impact on you, everyone around you, and your ultimate success.

Take Time to Get a Fresh Perspective

It is so easy for us to get caught up in the day-to-day process of running and managing our businesses that we lose perspective. And when we do, we fall into the trap of doing things the way we always have. I like to think about it this way...

The higher up you are in your organization, the greater the percentage of time you should spend working on your business, not working in your business.

A functional manager, someone who manages a call center for example, can perhaps spend 95% of the day supervising subordinates, tracking calling activity, and handling the other day-to-day requirements of the job. That would leave 5% of the day to reflect on how to do the job, make improvements, etc. But if you are a CEO, you should spend 95% of your time reflecting on your business considering what is happening in other industries, talking to senior executives at other companies, talking to customers and your senior executives and performing higher-level activities. If you are a middle manager, depending on the nature of your responsibilities, you might be able to invest 10% of your time reflecting on bigger issues and 90% of your time performing your job. The higher you are up on the company hierarchy, the more time you should spend working *on*, not in.

There are many ways to discover fresh perspectives. Regularly explore the marketplace—physically and through magazines, journals, and online. The concepts that you discover can be game changing.

Traveling to other countries can also open your eyes to new approaches. When I was in the floor covering business, for example, I got many ideas when I travelled to Europe. I saw that stores there did things quite differently from the way we did in the U.S.; I found ideas that had validity back home.

Another important activity is to look at competition not just in your space, but at companies in other industries that are courting the customers that you are. You are selling products that require those customers to spend dollars, but those customers also have the choice to spend their money in other ways. So, if you look closely at what companies are doing in other industries and sectors, you can develop new ideas about how you can compete for those dollars. Your millennial and Generation Z workers can be a source of information in these areas.

Ask for Input

Truly strong leaders are always asking questions and learning—they are not arrogant or autocratic.

Asking for input is a bit different from asking for help. When you ask for input, you are not asking for one-time assistance with a challenge, you are soliciting a wider range of ideas and suggestions on larger issues and topics.

Nothing is more critical than getting others involved in the larger processes on which you are working. There are many settings in which you can ask for input, including town-hall-style meetings, strategic planning sessions, councils that convene periodically, and surveys.

When you actively invite input, incredibly positive things happen. People will:

- Develop a vested interest in your success
- See your request as a sign that you are confident in yourself and open to new ideas
- Become advocates and ongoing contributors, not occasional acquaintances
- Become vested in your successful outcomes
- Be more motivated to improve the quality of the ideas they suggest to you

When you ask people for input, they become more motivated to do whatever it takes to make sure you are successful; you can reap all those benefits by asking for input.

Fight Complacency ("Business is good, so I don't need to improve it.")

Complacency comes in a variety of forms. You can recognize it in statements like:

- "Business is good—I'd like it to keep going well, so I don't need to do anything."
- "If it ain't broke, don't fix it."

- "I'm making enough money; I don't need to make more."

I actually had someone tell me, "I don't need to raise my margins. I'm making enough money. I'd rather just give more to my customers." On the surface that sounds noble, but it isn't. Profits might seem like greed, but they're not. They're about growing and investing in your business. They're about protecting your job and your employees' jobs. Every business needs profits.

If you're suffering from this pitfall and believe your business is so good that you don't need to grow it, I urge you to shake things up a bit and shift your perspective.

Unfortunately, your competitors probably didn't get that same message that they are doing *well enough*. They are innovating and growing their businesses. That is one reason why you constantly have to work to make your business better.

Another temptation to become complacent:

Some people seem to believe that if they work harder, they will destroy their work-life balance. I am a very big believer in establishing a good work-life balance, but the reality is that you want your business to achieve all it can achieve.

I like to remember that even in a company that has become wildly successful, it is still possible for people to enjoy time with their families.

To summarize, work-life balance doesn't mean your business goes on hold so you can attend to personal pursuits. The reality is if your business is on hold, your business is going backwards; some other company is going to outperform you. You will then have a serious issue when your business encounters problems in the future. Leading an enterprise that is going downhill will have a way of doing more harm to your work-life balance than you believed possible.

ACTION STEP

Reflect on areas in which you may have become complacent.

Decide How Much Collaboration to Encourage, and When

As a leader, part of your job is to decide the level of collaboration that you will encourage in different circumstances:

- Large-scale collaboration – There are times when it makes sense to invite everyone in your organization to weigh in and collaborate. If you are making a new commitment to improving the ratings you are receiving for your customer service, for example, you will probably want to gather insights from your customer service representatives, salespeople, call center personnel, the dealers who sell your products, other people who are in contact with customers, and customers.

- Collaboration with specific internal teams – There are also times when you should decide to collaborate and get input from a limited number of people in your organization. For instance, the members of your top executive team, your sales managers, your IT and tech people, or other groups that possess the specific knowledge and experience that equip them with the necessary information to give insights into the process or change that you are considering.

- Collaboration with specific external teams – There may also be times when you want input and help from people outside your internal organization, such as groups of customers, dealers, or franchisees. Part of your job as a leader is to understand and invite the right people into different processes.

After gathering insights and information, there can also come a time when you, if you are the executive leader, make an autonomous decision to move ahead with something.

Most companies, after all, do not function like democracies where everyone gets to vote on all big-picture issues. There may come a time when individuals who are practicing the art of leadership need to make calculated decisions to move ahead.

ACTION STEP

Review how you have collaborated on specific tasks and projects in the past. Did you involve the right people? If you could attack the same issue or challenge again, would you invite the same people to collaborate with you? If not, whom would you invite instead?

Build Ingagement through Participation

We often hear people say, "If we did everything by committee, we'd never get anything done." While there may be some truth to that, consider this statement: "If we never got input from people, think of all the mistakes we would make."

Genuine participation in pivotal projects and processes is one of the keys to success. Encouraging people to participate and plan projects (especially those that affect them directly) can help improve the level of Ingagement within any organization. Here are some steps you can take to encourage participation:

- Consider everyone to be a stakeholder – Talk to people, ask them how they would address problems, listen, and strive to understand the issue from their perspective. Remember, the more involved they are in a project, the more they will be invested in its success.

- Use task forces and idea committees to promote innovation – Create steering committees of thought leaders within your organization to get input and insight on important issues. Encourage people to ask, "How does this initiative help us get us closer to achieving our organization's goals?" and, "How does it align with our mission, vision and values?"

- Look for opportunities for managers and employees to participate in the communication process – Encourage them to contribute articles and other resources, invite feedback on the information they provide, share information, conduct polls and to be proactive in communication within your organization.

Have the Courage to Allow People to Take Risks

I believe it is important to let people take risks. Sometimes, however, those risks can carry the possibility of failure.

I know that sounds counterintuitive, and you are probably asking, "Are you really suggesting that if I know that one of my managers is going to do something wrong, I should let that person go ahead and fail? Why does that make any sense at all?"

I believe that it often does make sense to allow people to try things that you do not agree with, or that you have seen fail in the past. Though allow me to inject a note of caution here: As a leader, your job is to assess the risk in different situations and decide about where and when to apply the philosophy of letting people try risky things. You would not allow your managers to fail in extremely important activities where the consequences of failure would be too great.

Nonetheless, here are several compelling reasons for allowing your managers to take risks:

- First, if you always protect people from making mistakes, they will never develop the confidence to do anything on their own. They will never have the gumption to try brave new things, take risks, innovate, or accomplish results that are truly exceptional.

- Second, you reduce the risk of becoming a micromanager. When people have the autonomy to move ahead, they will not need to ask your permission to execute every small assignment that lies ahead. As a result, you will be able to let go of lower-level activities that should no longer occupy the time and attention of a higher-level executive.

- Third, you will never learn that some of your opinions could be wrong. Opinions, we know, tend to be flawed. Do you really know that all of yours are valid? Have you taken time to validate and research them? Have changes occurred in the world that you have not considered? Perhaps changes that could make your opinions outdated? If you allow people to move ahead even though you recognize a risk of failure, you will be amazed at how many times they will surprise you by succeeding. One example: An employee in marketing approaches you and says that he intends to run an advertisement in a particular publication, and you want to say, "I ran an ad there five years ago, and it failed miserably. Don't do it." But if you have the courage to let him run that ad, you might learn that changes have occurred that will cause the advertisement to succeed. Perhaps your products or services now have a more competitive advantage in the marketplace. Perhaps the readership of the publication has changed and more of your targeted customers are reading it today. Perhaps your product has become the only one of its kind that is produced domestically, and potential customers are eager to buy products that are made in America.

The bottom line is that when you ride in and prevent people from taking actions you believe are risky, you eliminate the possibility that they will bring something new and better to your enterprise. They might have a new twist on an old idea, or they might try something in a slightly different way. If you prevent them from trying, you only prevent them from finding some new kind of success.

Cultivate Positive Reflection, Not "Yes People"

The term "Yes Person" describes someone who says "Yes" to everything; who always agrees with you. If you are in a position of power and you're not actively seeking Ingaged collaboration from your staff and team, there is a real risk that your people will become "Yes People." They will sometimes knowingly follow a directive that will harm the company instead of pushing back and asking questions. That road clearly leads to reduced effectiveness and even potential failure. You want to develop a team that will contribute to find better outcomes.

If you don't feel your staff contributes a lot of ideas or asks questions when they're asked to execute something, then you are most likely creating "Yes People." Asking for opinions takes more time, but the investment you make will result in better ideas. Plus, your employees will be more supportive in making important things happen.

Take Time to Cultivate Repeat and Referral Business

There's a saying which goes, "Your next most likely customer is your last customer."

That statement is normally true, but there is more to it than that because your current best customers offer you the best opportunities to grow your business. You can do more business with them, and they can refer new customers to you.

If you are not devoting enough attention to cultivating repeat and referral business, you are limiting your opportunities to grow.

Here are some steps to take:

- **Identify your key top customers.** To find out who your top customers are, be sure to speak with your salespeople, customer service representatives and other people on the front lines.

- Start an ongoing conversation with them. Ask how you can improve your business with these customers.

- Ask them if they can introduce you to businesses that would benefit from working with you or buying from you. In most cases, they will be happy to do so.

I think you'll be surprised and delighted to see how happy your customers will be to help you grow your business; customers like to help. They also likely know that if they refer new customers to you, you will be motivated to return the favor by being more helpful to them.

It all starts by simply pinpointing who your best customers are and starting a conversation with them.

Keep Lines of Communication Open with Your Vendors

It's extremely tempting to look at a vendor as little more than someone who sells you stuff. However, if you can change that mindset and see vendors as partners, they can become a great source of information and knowledge that can support your efforts to build Ingagement.

It all starts with soliciting ideas and input from vendors, but you might not want to work in that way with all your vendors. It pays to consider your vendors and invite those who will be most likely to bring good things into a closer collaboration. One good approach is to resolve to work more closely with vendors whom you already have deep, positive relationships.

Like your customers, your vendors can offer you important insights, including:

- Front-line information about trends, news, and technology in your industry

- Objective opinions about what your organization is doing and what it needs to do

- Important intelligence about how people see your company in comparison to your competitors, and maybe even some important insight into what those competitors are planning and doing

Gaining such benefits starts by simply asking vendors to offer you input and advice.

Cultivate the Ability to "Eat Elephants"

You have probably heard the old question, "How do you eat an elephant?" The answer: "One bite at a time."

The answer to that question is a good one to keep in mind every day as a leader and a manager. Instead of feeling overwhelmed by the enormity of certain critical initiatives or processes that you would like to tackle, simply get started by taking a small step—in effect, by "taking one small bite at a time."

Those big elephants are the projects that seem so complex you tend to put them off. One could be writing a business plan for a new company or division that you would like to launch, so that you can obtain funding. Another might be studying the efficiencies of the outsourced call centers you are using so that you can decide whether to open an internal call center of your own.

When we are faced with tasks like those, "taking a first bite" is critically important. That bite could be creating an internal task force to explore an issue or calling some of your contacts to ask for input.

The first bite can be small, but here's one piece of advice that I can offer: Whatever that first bite will be, try to take it soon. Do it today, if possible.

ACTION STEP

Pinpoint a large project or initiative that you have been delaying. Make a list of small first "bites" you can take that can get the process started, then take action on one of them.

Concluding thoughts for this chapter:

As you have read this chapter, did any of its concepts "speak" to you? Did anything strike you as an area where you could improve, or an area that would offer significant returns if you addressed them? Chances are that some of them did. If this is the case, I'd encourage you to focus on them in the days and weeks ahead. As you have noticed in your work and career, people who continuously work to improve themselves, their teams, and their organizations become highly effective leaders.

CHAPTER SEVEN

Understanding and Communicating Your Company's Identity and Purpose

Every organization has a purpose and stands for something. Whether you're an executive or a manager, your ability to lead becomes vastly more effective when you understand just what that purpose is and use it to Ingage and inspire those around you.

Ingaging Leadership

Sometimes the seeds of a company's identity are sown by the founder or by a group of individuals who started the organization. But no identity is static, and over time it evolves as it is affected by new company leaders, employees, new company initiatives, trends in the marketplace and even by competitors.

No matter how your organization has evolved, your ability to be an Ingaged leader relies on your willingness to understand and define who you are, and to communicate that identity to people inside and outside your organization. Remember that members of the younger generations like to know that they are not just working but bringing value to the community and changing the world.

So, who are *you*? That knowledge comes from considering questions like:

- What do we stand for?

- Where have we been?

- Where are we going?

- What makes us unique?

- How are we perceived as a company?

- What is it about our company that makes people want to work here and build their future with us?

Let's dig a bit deeper by considering some of the traits of positive and negative company cultures.

Organizations with positive company cultures often:

- Have a high level of ethics

- Are committed to community, the environment, and other like values (i.e., a sustainability mindset)

- Enjoy an atmosphere of teamwork and camaraderie

- Have a shared sense of community

- Encourage creativity and thrive on innovation

- Promote risk-taking

- Are customer-focused

- Keep employees' families in mind and promote a positive work/life balance

- Foster a positive approach and sense of fun

- Provide generous benefits
- Encourage employees' personal and professional development
- Embrace continuous learning
- Create opportunities for growth and advancement
- Have strong and shared core values
- Promote technological innovation
- Are fiscally realistic

Walk into a company with a positive culture and you will see happy, relaxed people working hard and without tension. You'll hear people who are sharing ideas, consulting each other, and laughing. There is a sense of openness, and you will feel relaxed and welcome.

Organizations with negative company cultures often:

- Maintain false communication where everyone "weighs in," yet few feel heard and results are delayed
- Neglect collaboration
- Ignore unhealthy and, in some cases illegal behavior

such as sexism, male dominance, racism, intolerance, emotional and physical abuse

- Disregard disruptive internal competition and sniping

- Suffer from minimal employee loyalty

- Lose time and money to low productivity and high turnover

- Have unnecessary hierarchies

- Lack a healthy life/work balance

- Tend to be rigid and continue to do things "the way we've always done them"

When you visit a company with a poor corporate culture, tension permeates every level. You will see grim faces, and you will likely notice many offices with closed doors. You may feel uncomfortable, without knowing why. The reason

ACTION STEP

Take some time and review the factors that create company culture. Where does your current company culture belong among the categories that we mentioned above? Where would you like it to be? What changes will you make to get there?

you may feel uncomfortable is because everyone who works there is uncomfortable and disconnected.

It Takes Positive People to Create a Positive Culture

We will explore the issue of staffing in depth in Chapter Seven. At this point in the book, let me simply observe that as you clarify your vision for what you want your culture to become over time, it will become clearer to you whether you have the right people on board to support that culture; you might come to some surprising conclusions. I know one organization, for example, that had to come face-to-face with the realization that some of its more profit-producing staff members, and the most valued, were individuals who did not like to share ideas openly with other people. Yet even if you discover something troubling about your staffing, over time you can build toward the culture you want through transformative activities like:

- Hiring. Recruit people who possess the traits and outlooks that support the culture you want to build. Once you define the culture you want to create and start building it, more of the right people will discover you and want to work for you.

- Compartmentalizing. Remember that it is generally

not necessary for every employee to embody everything that you want your company culture to be. If a manufacturer is developing a culture of creativity, for example, it might be more critical to encourage that trait in product designers and marketers than in product assemblers. You do, however, want to have people in key leadership and management positions who are committed to the values you want to achieve.

- Coaching and training. Some people find it very difficult to change less-than-ideal behaviors that have proved to be successful. Although, as a leader or influential manager, you have more ability to influence people than you might expect.

Be Forward-Thinking and Envision What You Want to Become

It is sometimes worthwhile to ask, "So what did we do in the past that worked? Why don't we bring it back?" Sometimes this approach works, but always reaching back to what worked in the past is generally not expanding your growth. After all, future trends and changes will influence who you become as an organization.

Few leaders—even excellent ones—can predict the future with complete accuracy. However, certain questions will help you get a vision of how you will evolve in the years ahead:

- How have our customers changed and what does that tell me about how they could change in the future?

- Are there technological changes that we will have to adopt in order to thrive?

- What is the projected life of our offerings? Are they still competitive? At what point will we need to discontinue them, alter them, or upgrade them in order to stay competitive?

- How might our competitors fare in the years ahead? Are they growing stronger or weaker? What are their key competitive advantages and disadvantages against us?

ACTION STEP

Reflect on the business you are in and make a list of predictions about the changes that are about to happen in your industry in the next five years.

Practical Ways to Define Who You Are, So You Can Communicate Your Culture and Plans More Effectively

I recommend creating several working documents that help you understand and communicate where you *are* and where you *are going* as an organization.

Create a Mission Statement

A mission statement is a short, succinct statement that tells all your stakeholders—your leadership team, your employees, your customers and the world—who you are and what you do. In the case of my consulting company, our mission is "We are Ingagement champions. We help our clients succeed by helping them build strong, Ingaged organizations."

Create a Vision Statement Too

A vision statement is different from a mission statement in that a vision statement describes what you want your organization to *become* in a larger sense. In our case, we want to be the world's most widely recognized and respected thought leaders in the field of Ingaged Leadership and management.

As you consider the vision for your organization and decide how to communicate it, it can be a good idea to benchmark against renowned individuals and companies with strong and compelling visions. For example, Tom Peters immediately comes to mind when someone mentions business excellence, thanks to his book written in 1982, *In Search of Excellence*. Stephen R. Covey is top-of-mind when the philosophy of effective leadership is mentioned; he came to national attention in 1989 with the publication of his first book, *The 7 Habits of Highly Effective People*.

What will you and your organization become? What are your biggest hopes and aspirations? What you desire to attain should form the core of your vision statement.

Be sure to Ingage other people in the process of defining and refining your vision.

That can mean resisting the temptation to develop it in the vacuum of a senior management meeting.

CASE STUDY

How Chipotle Defines its Mission and Vision

Chipotle, one of the hottest restaurant chains on the American landscape today, frames its mission and vision this way:

- Chipotle's mission (what the company does) is to "*serve food with integrity.*"

- Chipotle's vision (its aspiration for what it will become) is to "*change the way people think about fast food.*"

Communicate Who You Are in a Strategic Way

I recommend that you communicate your mission, vision statement, and strategic plan purposefully.

What do I mean by purposefully? I mean sharing your planning documents with your employees, and also with key customers and suppliers, provided they play a large and significant role in your success. You might also want to share certain parts of your plan on your website—though not your full long-range plan.

Some people will question the wisdom of sharing internal documents too freely. They wonder how wise it is to let your competitors see so much information about your company and your plans, and I understand and respect such an argument. Though at the same time, how can you go somewhere when your team doesn't know where you are going, your vendors don't know, and your customers don't know?

In my experience, it would be highly unlikely for a competitor to steal your plans and use them more successfully than you can. Your competitors, after all, have their own plans, agendas, and challenges to address; they are only as effective as their ability to execute their own plans. Just because your competition can see your mission, vision, and plan doesn't mean they can execute them.

Refine Your Vision through Long-Term Planning

It is crucial to push yourself to think long-term, not short-term. That might sound like a complex and difficult process, but you can get started by asking some fundamental questions:

- If I were starting fresh and wanted to start an enterprise that would put my own organization out of business, what exact steps would I take?

- If I were starting again and wanted to open a business that would put *everyone* else out of business, what exact steps would I take?

Those questions will help you identify some of the critical things you should be doing and eliminate the minutiae details that are probably claiming most of your time now. Make a list of the biggest and most ambitious issues you are facing, then determine if it is possible to solve them—and when, and how. Such a list can help you create a vision for your company and identify specific challenges and tasks that can help you grow into a much more successful organization.

Let Your Customers Help Define Who You Are

It's important that you understand what your customers do and how what you do affects them. In turn, you will then be a better partner to them and will also:

- Gain valuable end-user generated, real-world insights

- Avoid developing tunnel vision and groupthink

- Stay grounded because customers tell you things about

your organization that are very hard to learn anywhere else

You can connect directly with individuals from a cross-section of your customer base or invite them to working meetings. Stress that their assistance will strengthen your relationship and lead to shared benefits. Including customers in this process is always productive.

How Customers Helped One Organization Grow

After I got my MBA, I went to work in my family business. We had a solid business, but its growth was completely stalled. For three years in a row it had done $3 million in volume. There seemed to be no way to break that cycle, but we did. In fact, we went from $3 million to $5 million to $10 million to $25 million in four years' time.

How did we accomplish those phenomenal results? We invited both our employees and customers into the process. Our company had five divisions, and after consulting each one, we created a business plan and a vision statement for each division.

Our customers contributed insights about how we could work better with them and be much more customer-responsive than we had been before. Additionally, since our employees felt they were an important part of the process too, implementing the plan went smoothly.

Our plan predicted that we would grow from $3 million to $10 million in five years. In fact, we went from $3 million to $25 million in only four. With our customers as our partners, we were wildly successful at growing the business.

Create a Strategic Plan to Get to Where You Want to Go

A strategic plan is an important tool that can help your organization grow, achieve specific goals on a schedule, and reach its fullest potential. To define the goals and timelines that will be part of your plan, you will need to consult with your management team, appropriate managers and employees, vendors, customers and other stakeholders as well. Remember that a strategic plan should be grounded in your company's vision and mission statements, which reflect your values, goals and aspirations.

How far ahead should you be planning? Five years into the future is normally ideal. Your goals should be challenging and stretch you, while also being concrete and straightforward. Goals that lie 10 or 20 years into the future become so esoteric that people cannot relate to them.

Now, are you really going to use one plan, accomplish everything that is in it, and then meet again in five years to write a new one? No, not likely. I recommend creating a five-year plan, meeting at least once a year to review it, and ask some questions:

- Where are we now in executing this plan?

- Do we still want to pursue all the goals that it sets out, or have other priorities emerged that we should tackle first?

- What specific tactics do we need to work on in the next year so that we can accomplish our goals?

The *status quo* changes quickly in business today, and while you will need to revise your plan and keep your goals fresh, there is great value in saying to people, "Here are our goals for the next five years." This is especially true when you create specific initiatives, assignments, and tactics that people will address in the year to follow.

Here's an analogy that illustrates the importance of planning:

If you put 22 kids who have never played soccer before on a soccer field and you said to them, "Here's a soccer ball, have fun playing soccer," what kind of soccer game would it be? They wouldn't necessarily know there were two teams. They wouldn't know the rules or how to keep score. They might eventually start kicking the ball around, but the actual game of soccer wouldn't happen. However, when you explain the game and that the goal is to kick the ball into the net, then people achieve and accomplish something.

The same is true in business. When you're just doing the same things over again and no one has given you a goal or a plan—no one has told you how to score—you just keep doing the same things repeatedly. You don't know what you should be doing and it's impossible to achieve any kind of success.

Concluding thoughts for this chapter:

As the Roman philosopher Seneca once wrote, "If a sailor does not know to which port he is sailing, no wind is favorable." In other words, to get to the right place you must know what you and your organization want to achieve; that means defining your mission, vision and goals.

CHAPTER EIGHT

Communication Skills for Ingaged Leadership

The single biggest problem in communication is the illusion that it has taken place.

- George Bernard Shaw

Even the greatest techniques for Ingaged Leadership will not be effective until you communicate clearly and compellingly. Throughout this chapter, we will look at how to do just that.

Most managers and top executives know that it takes a lot of work to communicate clearly. It requires:

- Effectively conveying the big picture

- Considering the people you are speaking with, their ages, concerns and sense of identity

- Motivating people to participate and deliver their very best

- Communicating just the right amount of information—neither too much nor too little

- Sending the right messages to your teams

- Conveying instructions and ideas clearly

- Ingaging people in the process decision-making, not just telling them what to do

- Helping people understand not just *what* to do, but *why* they are doing it

Analyze Your Communications

How can you know if your company has good communications? Here are some signs to watch for in employees and managers:

- An eagerness to communicate – The staff enjoys and is enthusiastic about planning, meetings, simple conversations, and the memos and communications that they receive from others in your organization.

- Smooth communication – Team members, managers and employees receive, understand, and act on the information they receive. There is minimal need to repeat messages. People access your intranet, read your communications, and stay Ingaged. As a result, top executives can Ingage in higher-level pursuits like long-term planning, product development, and cultivating new markets and customers.

- Ambition and enterprise – People are eager to get going on new initiatives, get work done, and help in the pursuit of organizational excellence.

- Widespread understanding of bigger issues – People

don't only know what's happening on a daily basis, they also understand the company's long-term goals, mission, vision and values. They take an active role in helping the company succeed.

- **Ability to execute** – People don't only start projects, they finish them. Few to no people do just enough to "get by."

- **Confidence and empowerment** – People believe in themselves, feel supported by management, and complacency has not set in.

Why Poor Communication Is Costly

According to "The High Cost of Poor Communication," a report from the 360 Solutions consulting organization, poor communication patterns are both costly and frustrating. The study found that in a company with 100 employees where inefficient communication patterns have taken hold, company leadership has to invest an average of 17 hours each week to clarify communication. That translates to an annual company cost of $528,443.

According to the study, some of the costliest forms of poor communication can be traced to closed-minded leaders who cut off feedback. The result being a company culture that tolerates interruptions, negative body language, and even anger.

Keys to Building More Ingaged Personal Communication

Some of us start out as poor communicators and must work hard to improve, while many of us start around the middle levels; very few of us start out as highly effective communicators. But where we start is less important than our desire to improve our abilities.

How can you cultivate the habit of continuous improvement as a communicator? Here are some attitudes to think about, cultivate, and apply strategically:

- When appropriate, start with no dependence on achieving a specific outcome. Instead, intend for the highest good to come about. Remaining focused on specific outcomes can distract you from achieving a higher good.

- Be curious to hear more, know more, and to help others learn.

- Ask open-ended questions that require more than a "yes" or "no" reply.

- Probe the statements and answers that you hear to get a full understanding. Don't assume you know what someone else means.

- Try to consider where other people are coming from, what is at stake for them, and ask questions to understand what their unspoken concerns may be.

- Distinguish fact from opinion. (We will explore this issue in more depth in Chapter Five.)

- Be mentally present to ensure that you understand what you're hearing.

- Be conscious when you are triggered (upset or angry) and learn to quickly set those feelings aside. Then, return to your search for good ideas and solutions.

- Take the time to notice how others react to what you say.

- Strive for solutions that meet the needs of many people.

- Be patient in your communication and allow others to speak at a pace that is most natural to them.

Five Ways to Make People More Receptive to What You Are Saying

I once worked with an organization that distributed a recorded audio clip to its entire sales force. At the end of the recording, salespeople were asked to send an email to a specific administrative assistant. Each salesperson who listened to the entire clip until the end would learn that he or she had received a watch—and a pretty nice watch at that. Yet only two out of the 800 salespeople responded to that offer; they were the only ones who listened to the entire message. The rest of the salesmen and saleswomen didn't get that far. Unfortunately, this is a common problem.

Here are some strategies that will help ensure your employees are interested and involved in what you have to say:

- Understand and communicate the "What's In It For Me" (WIIFM) – People are more likely to read communications or act on them when they perceive a clear and immediate benefit from doing so.

- Explain the "why" – People will be more likely to act if they understand the reasons behind your communication.

- Keep emails and other communications clear and simple – Be organized, to the point.

- Resist the temptation to repeat yourself unnecessarily – People are far less likely to open or read your communications if they know that you will convey the same information consistently.

- Define roles and responsibilities – Clearly state who is on the team and explain their respective responsibilities.

Remember that performance reviews offer a good opportunity to evaluate each employee's skills as a communicator. If people need to improve or refine their skills, find workshops or professional educational courses that will help them.

The Junk Drawer Analogy

Do you have an intranet or communication portal for information, updates, company news, and the like? If so, pay special attention that information is current, brief, clear and worth reading.

Sadly, communication portals can easily resemble the "junk drawer" that many of us use as a place to put stuff that we don't want to deal with. You know what that drawer is like—it contains what seems like everything but finding what you're looking for can waste a lot of time. Sometimes you may have to empty the entire contents, only to discover that what you're looking for isn't even there.

Keep the "Junk Drawer Analogy" in mind when arranging communications within your organization. If you keep things uncluttered and simple, you will save a lot of time, improve efficiency, and enjoy many other dividends.

Take Pains to Differentiate Fact from Opinion

This is a very critical issue for me. We are living in a time when many people express their opinions as if they were facts; many do it unknowingly, others intentionally. We hear politicians do it, and it has also become commonplace on talk radio and television news.

When people speak with any level of passion or conviction, they often speak as if what they are saying is fact. Realistically, much of what people try to pass off as facts are simply opinions. When people state an opinion as a fact, their audience is prone to believe it to be a fact, and thus, react to it in a certain way. Most often, the conversation either ends or never gets to the point of addressing real issues.

You might hear someone in your organization say, for example, "You cannot bring that product to market by early next year because of 'A, B, and C.'" That person is stating opinions as though they were facts and if you disagree, you look like you are calling him or her a liar.

If you cultivate the habit of delineating between fact and opinion during conversations, you become more empowered to move toward real solutions. If you fail to do so, miscommunications result. Imagine, for example, that you're asking for advice about an issue, but you express your opinion of that situation as though it were an undisputable truth. In such a case, the advice that you receive will probably not have great merit because the other person will not base his or her advice on a wider and more comprehensive understanding of what the situation really is.

From the other side of the equation, it is wise to cast a similarly critical eye on the information you receive by consistently challenging the assumption that what is being said or presented to you is actually fact. To make the most informed decisions, you need to investigate and become certain that you are not assessing opinions, but the reality of what is taking place.

Now, it's not realistic to think you can do this with absolutely everything that comes across your desk or in every conversation. Time limitations and pressures will often keep you from probing deeply into what you are hearing. And you do not need to do so all the time—not when you are dealing with low-priority issues or activities, for example, like an employee who usually arrives late to work or a salesperson who failed to file his weekly reports on time last week. But when you are dealing with serious issues, you'll want to dig deeper—to look at every angle to get to the real facts.

When you get there, you'll realize a significant improvement in business. Fact or opinion? You decide.

Communications skills that help differentiate opinions from facts:

- When you are offering an opinion, precede it with the phrase, "In my opinion..." This differentiates opinions from facts. Perhaps more importantly, it raises the quality of the conversation by inviting people to contribute to your opinion, refute it, or offer productive alternatives of their own.

- Ask other people, "Is what you are saying a fact or an opinion?" This strategy, like the one above, encourages others to be more alert to situations in which they are tempted to offer their opinions as facts.

- Point out when other people are presenting opinions as facts. This can be difficult to do because in a way, you are pointing out that those other people might be lying; it can be unpleasant to challenge other people's opinions. If someone says, for example, "Your price increases are killing sales," you should consider exposing that statement by stating that it is an opinion, not a fact. You can then explore that opinion to see if it has validity or is simply an attempt to box you into a corner or limit a productive search for information and solutions. In some cases, you will discover the other person is simply trying to advance his or her own agenda or goals. One good choice of words is to say, "I believe . . ." ("I believe that other factors could be at work too . . . let's explore some more.") In a non-confrontational way, an "I believe" statement can help you address the reality that another person is expressing an opinion as though it were a fact.

- Get into the habit of looking for facts. If someone says, "Your price increases are killing sales," you can work with that person to arrive at statistics, data, feedback, and facts that either support or refute the opinion. This elevates the quality of your conversation to a level of higher Ingagement.

ACTION STEP

Over the next two days, pay attention to times when people state opinions as facts. Watch some commentary shows on television and notice when it's taking place. Pay attention to your own communication too, and try to make sure that others know when you are stating an opinion. What do these steps tell you about how effectively you and other people in your organization make this important distinction?

Fight the Tendency to Make Assumptions when Communicating

As executives, we are often pressured to find immediate solutions to problems that we are facing. We therefore must fight the natural temptation to make quick assumptions.

For example, we tend to have preconceived notions about the effectiveness of what we are doing, often based on what has been effective in the past. If staffers aren't complaining about our management style or systems, we assume that people like them. By the same token, we tend to make assumptions about what other people are doing. If sales are going well, we assume the people we have hired are doing a good job of selling.

Yet we can challenge our assumptions and encourage others to follow suit. I am not talking about micromanaging, I am stressing the importance of remaining aware and hands-on as an executive or manager, in appropriate and involved ways. How do we remain aware? Keep talking, reviewing, and communicating with the people in your organization. Consistent and Ingaged communication is key, and here is one beneficial way to achieve it . . .

Invest Energy to Become a Good Listener

Are you a good listener? A "real" good listener? Or do distracting thoughts make your mind wander during meetings? Do you become defensive and tend to find fault with others? Are you a selective listener, looking to prove that others are wrong, and you are right?

A good way to overcome those inhibitors is to be *purposeful* in your conversation by building these skills:

- **Remain mentally present during conversations.** Focus your attention closely on what the other person is saying and how he or she is saying it.

- **Don't interrupt or rush to reply.** Be sure the other person is finished speaking before you respond. It is helpful to take a breath while considering your next comment instead of speaking completely off the cuff. This is especially important when discussing sensitive or emotional topics.

- **Acknowledge the positive and useful point that is being made.** Then build on it by digging deeper.

- **Analyze communications that have taken place.** Consider what went well, what could have gone better, and how to improve next time.

When you do these things, you will have better conversations, deeper relationships, and better outcomes. You will spend more time looking for the little nuggets of high value during your conversations and use them to stay focused on positive results.

ACTION STEP

Talk to some trusted friends to determine if you are a good listener. Rather than asking them whether your listening skills are good, ask some open-ended questions like, "After we have discussed something, do you feel as though I have heard you out, or do you still have ideas that you were not able to air?" or, "When you are speaking, do I allow you enough time and space to fully explain what is on your mind?" After those open-ended questions, consider asking something more direct, like, "Can you recommend two or three specific things I could do if I wanted to become a better listener?"

Concluding thoughts for this chapter:

As you have read this chapter, have you discovered any areas where you need to improve as a communicator? Every small improvement that you make in the effectiveness of your communication will quickly repay you with remarkable and rewarding improvements. Both your leadership skills and your organization will benefit.

CHAPTER NINE

Mastering the Three Types of Communication

The best leaders and managers don't let their communication just "happen." They adapt their style of communication to achieve desired outcomes.

I n this chapter, we will explore a new way to think about the process of communication—a way of thinking that that can lead to more Ingaged and effective leadership.

I will present a way to understand and explore three distinct types of communication. Why am I devoting an entire chapter to three levels of communication that I have identified? Let me explain. When you learn to recognize the three types of communication:

- You will be in a better position to understand the people you lead. If people are being evasive and covering up information, for example, you will be better able to discern such is taking place. Even more importantly, you will be in a better position to understand their motivations, to lift their communication to a higher level, and to lead them in a more insightful and Ingaging manner.

- You will become a more genuine, positive, and Ingaged leader. I believe that when leaders distort the truth (which is a kinder way of saying they are lying), they damage their own ability to lead in many ways that are not immediately apparent. If you develop the habit of telling small lies, like telling people that their reports are due tomorrow when next week is time enough, you might not get caught telling a lie. But over time, your authenticity as a leader will erode because people's intuition will subtly alert them that you are not as authentic a leader as you once seemed to be. Getting in the habit of distorting the truth, omitting information, and engaging in other small forms of lying can also weaken your resolve to lead on the highest, most ethical level.

When you take extra effort to understand what other people are saying, you will communicate much more effectively and build more Ingaged Leadership. In a sense, this chapter's content is an extension of the communication skills that we explored in the previous chapter, though these additional concepts are so important they deserve a chapter of their own.

Type 1 – Evasive Communication

Most of the communication that takes place in this category has to do with lying. There are three subcategories of communication that take place within Evasive Communication:

- **Straight-out lying** – When people communicate in this way, their actions show an attitude of, "I lie habitually, without provocation."

- **Defensive lying** – "When I am being questioned or feel threatened, I lie to cover myself. I often do it without much thought; it just happens."

- **Withholding information (not telling the whole truth)** – "I am avoiding certain topics, or not responding or contributing pertinent information when someone else is talking with me." This most often occurs when someone is trying to influence a conversation so that it results in a decision that he or she prefers.

Despite the fact that this is seemingly the least effective type of communication, there are still times when positive leaders adapt it to save time. Many of those times are rooted in customs—the ways we habitually interact in our society.

Let's say, for example, that a colleague comes into my office one day and asks, "How are you?" It so happens that I am not feeling too well that day. But there is no good reason to say, "Since you asked, I have a headache, I think I might be getting a cold, and I am grumpy." Alternatively, in the interest of efficiency, I will likely just answer, "Doing ok, felt better," and then get into the substance of our meeting. We all take part in this kind of communication every day, in which it is pointless and time-wasting to respond with complete honesty.

At the same time, it is crucial to think carefully and critically before choosing to omit or shape information to achieve certain results. For example, I have known salespeople who called into their companies and lied about the orders they place. One told his company that a client "Needed to have his order delivered by the end of the month," when in fact, the customer had never made that demand. This salesperson wanted the order to be delivered so he could make his monthly sales quota and earn a commission on the sale sooner.

You might think there was no harm in what that salesperson did—he lied to reach certain goals. Yet what would have happened if his lie were uncovered? For example, what if the customer called the salesperson's supervisor and said that he had never requested a delivery by month's end? The salesperson's credibility and reputation would have been destroyed, both with his client and with his company. It is always wisest to look at how you are communicating and ask, "Can this lie cause damage?"

Consider the damage that results when people within an organization get in the habit of lying defensively to protect themselves. Unfortunately, this is not uncommon. Someone fails to notice an email, therefore fails to execute an important project, and thus tells everyone, "I never got that email."

Or perhaps someone forgets to make an important phone call and later lies, "I left a message, but nobody returned my call."

Let's face it—at one time or another, it's tempting to stretch the truth or avoid it altogether to sidestep blame. This behavior can do more harm than you might expect; severe operational problems take root in companies where lying has become commonplace. The real and deeper problem is that in such organizations, management becomes cut off from what's really going on and cannot respond to problems that should be addressed.

Although in some cases "white lies" of withholding information may seem benign, that's not always the case. This is another reason why it is so important to uncover, evaluate, and influence communication in your organization.

Quick assessment exercise

- Can you think of a time when you practiced evasive communication? Did you do so intentionally, or by force of habit? What were the results?

- Can you think of a time when someone else practiced evasive communication? What happened, and were the outcomes good or bad?

ACTION STEP

When have you been evasive and why? What was the result? Remember, there are times when withholding information can be practical. It is not necessary to share every detail of information in every situation, after all. Be aware, however, that people who are habitually evasive – who constantly try to "cover their backs"– can do a lot of harm to your organization.

Type 2 – Conclusive Communication

If I am participating in communication of this type, I am speaking honestly. However, I am not communicating authentically because I am trying to direct the conversation and achieve a specific result. I am shaping the way I communicate because I have unspoken goals and motives that I am trying to advance.

There are three subcategories of communication within Conclusive Communication:

- Impulsive self-interest – When people communicate in this way, their actions show a distinct attitude: "I say what is on my mind without much thought or concern to the purpose of the conversation or interests of the person I am talking to. Many times, this happens when a conversation erupts before I have had a chance to think first about what I will say. I am supposed to be listening to the person I am talking to, but instead I am only concerned with what I am thinking." In other words, try to stop thinking about what you will reply or say next, and actively listen to what another person is saying.

- Defending a position or goal – "I am expressing my true thoughts and I understand the purpose of the conversation and the other person's desires and goals. However, I am not willing to truly consider anyone else's point of view. I am either fighting for my point of view or defending it."

- Seeking to blame and find fault – "I am asking good questions and acting like I truly care about the other person's point of view. However, my real goal is to use what the person is saying to either prove I have listened or to find ammunition to defeat his or her point of view. I am not really open to changing my mind; I just try to manipulate the person I am talking to."

As I wrote at the start of this chapter, applying those communications styles at the wrong times can diminish your authenticity and credibility as a leader. There are other times, however, when leaders must make the decision not to take part in completely open and receptive communication.

- Example One: Your company operations manual states that your company opens its door for business every day at 8:00 A.M. One day an employee arrives an hour late and says, "I feel tired; I think that starting tomorrow, we should begin opening our doors at 9:00." If that happens, my response as a manger will not be to say, "Please tell me why you think it would be better to start opening an hour later," and then engage in a lengthy discussion about it because in order for my company to continue doing business, we need to follow our operating procedures. (If your employees have a big meeting every year to review our procedures and norms, that is the place to discuss changing our hours of operation, not on a situational basis.)

- Example Two: As a manager, you need one of the people you supervise to do something in the next 20 minutes, like calling up a vendor to ask when an important shipment will arrive. You are not going to ask the employee, "Can you tell me in depth how you feel about calling the vendor?" Similarly, if your supervisor asks you to do something quickly, the best idea is probably just to do it. If you want to discuss the nature of the task or your job in more depth, you should pick another time.

- Example Three: Complete openness and honesty are sometimes not ideal when you are negotiating an agreement with someone whose goals are in opposition to yours. Let's say, for instance, that you and your attorneys are trying to negotiate a financial settlement with a company that has infringed on a patent you hold. You have your position, so does the other side, and it is not a time to ask questions like, "Tell me how you feel about paying us what we are owed." The people on the other side will undoubtedly be pressing for their own agenda and needs too, and your strong position can only benefit you.

Quick assessment exercise:

Can you think of a time when you took part in conclusive communication?

- If you have communicated in this way, was it intentional? If so, why?

- How useful were the outcomes?

- Who in your organization uses this type of communication, either habitually or occasionally? What effect are they having on your company culture, efficiency, and success?

Type 3 – Openness and Honesty

If I have reached this type of communication, I am speaking openly, without being tied to a result. I am willing to allow others' ideas and thoughts to play an equal part alongside mine in the conversation. Again, there are three subcategories of communication within this type of communication:

- Not fully involved in the process of changing my mind – When people communicate in this way, their actions show "I am fully honest in conversation, clearly creating a distinction between the facts and my opinions. I listen to what the other person has to say, but I stop short of pulling their whole thoughts from them. I am only somewhat open to changing my mind, not actively committed to the process of exchanging ideas and contributions."

- Willingness to change my mind – "I present facts first and then opinions. I clearly delineate the differences between the two, and I communicate with clarity. I am concerned for the other person's point of view. I ask open-ended questions to fully understand them, and I am fully open to a change in my opinion."

- Clarity and openness – "I go into conversations with no defined outcomes in mind, not even a preferred direction that I might be willing to change; I have a totally open mind. I concern myself not only with the statements that the other person is making, but I also try to understand the other person's underlying intent. I consider what is at stake for the person I am talking to and what his or her concerns and goals are. When I ask questions, I listen to the answers with true curiosity. I follow up on the answers I hear by asking deeper and more probing questions that help me fully understand the other person's point of view. I clearly delineate the difference between fact and my own opinion. I may get triggered (experience strong, unproductive feelings) when the other person states a position that differs from mine, but I am able to set my triggers aside; I know that their viewpoints are as legitimate as mine are, so I strive to find the fit between what they see and what I see. My goal is for the mutually best outcome."

This is a level of informed and active communication that is worth striving for in many situations. If I am interacting with a colleague whose input and ideas can lead to improved operations within my organization, I want to be at this level in my communication—not to get stuck at lower levels because of my own habits or those of the person I am working with.

When you are taking part in true leadership activities, you should be able to practice communication at this high level. Only through supremely evolved communication abilities can you lead an organization to achieve its fullest potential. But having mastered those communication skills, wise leaders know how to weigh and apply them in the service of efficiency and results.

Quick assessment exercise:

- Are you able to take part in open and honest communication? If not, can you pinpoint any roadblocks that are holding you back?

- If you have engaged in open and honest communication, were the outcomes good or bad?

- Are there people in your organization who take part in open and honest communication at this level, either habitually or occasionally? If so, what effect are they having on your company culture, efficiency, and success?

- If you were able to strategically achieve this level of communication within your organization, what do you believe the results would be?

ACTION STEP

Think of a conversation you had when you were conclusive – and when you could have benefitted from being more open and honest. If you could now repeat that talk at a higher level, how might the results have differed?

A Final Word on Communicating Effectively in the Three Types

I have observed that when it comes to communicating at these different levels, you get what you give, and you give what you get.

That is a way of saying that if you begin a conversation with someone using one of the types of communication that I describe in this chapter, he or she will tend to communicate with you at that same level. If I start a conversation at a level of conclusive communication, for example, the other person will tend to adopt that level as well. And if I start lying to protect myself, the other person will likely do the same. On the positive side, if I make a statement like, "I really want to hear your best ideas and suggestions. Do you have a few minutes to spend with me?" people will rise to that style of communication.

Concluding thoughts for this chapter:

Spend some time thinking about the concepts that we have covered in this chapter and the different types of communication that we have explored.

After I have explained them to executives and managers, most have told me shortly afterwards, that their effectiveness has immediately improved. They have saved time, motivated people more effectively, lowered the level of frustration that comes with inefficient communicating, and enjoyed other benefits. If you would like to experience a dramatic improvement in your leadership, the skills in this chapter are a good place to start.

CHAPTER TEN

Recruiting and Hiring Younger Generations

The steps that your company needs to take to hire people who are members of the younger generations are different from the steps you have traditionally followed when hiring people from older generations. Job applicants from the younger generations are looking to be inspired and have a clear understanding of the opportunity you are offering them. Having said that, let me add that hiring steps you use when recruiting members of the younger generations work great for all generations today.

What is the best way to hire younger generation workers? That is a very unintelligent question to ask, but a very intelligent one by contrast.

It is unintelligent because on a lot of levels, hiring younger generations is just like hiring anyone else. You define the job you need filled and pinpoint the skills and aptitudes that it takes to do the job. You run ads, network to find strong candidates, post the job in your company's job listings, and find ways to attract interest from potential job applicants. You give interviews, screen, check references, and follow the steps you can read about in any book on good hiring practices (we don't need to delve into them for you in this book). You follow a similar set of steps, whether you are recruiting younger generations, Baby Boomers, or anyone else.

That's why "What are the most effective ways to recruit strong younger generation workers?" is a dumb thing to ask. But it is a very intelligent question too as there are more specific things you need to focus on if you're going to be more effective in hiring younger generations.

When seeking to fill any job, there is always an element of selling involved—the art of convincing your strongest candidates to come on board after you have found them, and not to take other jobs they are considering.

In the old way of hiring new employees, job applicants sold themselves to companies. Today, that has changed. The applicant is still being interviewed, but today, the company is being interviewed too. When recruiting younger generations, hiring companies need to bear in mind that there are certain important attributes that younger generations are looking for; attributes like an exciting environment, a clear and understandable path to advancement, a chance to exercise personal autonomy while still being part of a stimulating team, and more.

The Traditional Process

The company advertises for positions on a job board. The applicants send in resumes and nicely worded cover letters that explain why they would be perfect for the job. All the applicants are reviewed, and a few are selected for the next step which is a phone interview. After the phone interviews, candidates are selected for face-to-face interviews.

In those interviews, candidates sell themselves to the company. Then the company may require some aptitude testing, drug testing, etc., and subsequently, job offers are made.

The process is fairly one-sided. The problem is, this process will generally not work well with members of younger generations; they are not stuck with the same pre-conceived notion that they shouldn't ask questions and just be happy that someone offered them a job. They are different. They want to know more about the company; what the company values. They want to understand their role and understand how to succeed and earn promotions.

ACTION STEP

Step back and devote some time to thinking about your hiring procedures and practices. Are they the best possible ones for getting younger professionals to apply?

The old model is one-sided—the new model needs to be two-sided if you want to hire the best and retain the best younger generational talent. I would argue these same techniques will improve the quality of hiring with every generation, including Baby Boomers.

Here are the keys.

Talk to Younger Generations About Your Company's Values and Mission

Generalizations tend to be...well, general. But the fact remains that most younger generations don't want to work for just any company; they hope to contribute their efforts and hours to a company that stands for something beyond making money. They want to share in the vision of your company, and they hope that working for your company will hold some importance in some way.

Set Out the Specifics

Younger generations like to have specifics spelled out. Even though they have earned a reputation for being "loosey-goosey" and casual, most of them are not. The more specific and concrete you get in setting out expectations and procedures, the more they will want to come on board.

Stress Autonomy, Creativity and Entrepreneurship

In general, younger generations like to *express* themselves through their jobs—not to be "cogs in a machine." They like to make decisions, implement plans, and make a personal, recognizable contribution to the companies for which they work.

Introduce Job Applicants to Future Supervisors and Team Members

Being part of a team is often more important to younger

generations than it is to Boomers or members of other age groups. For many younger generations, teamwork counts—despite their desire to be strong, recognized individuals.

Take Extra Care to Be Sure the Job Is a Good Fit

Why is it especially important to consider job fit when hiring younger generations? One obvious reason is that good fit helps assure members of the younger generations that they will perform well in their new jobs—that's a given. But there's a subtler reason; younger generations are generally less likely to stay in jobs that they find frustrating, overly difficult to perform, or repetitive and dull. With greater speed than Boomers, younger generations will quit jobs and move on quickly to other jobs.

That is not because younger generations lack company loyalty or are "job hoppers." It is because they want to enjoy a sense of progress, skill, and accomplishment in their daily work. If you hire them and they leave you soon after, you will have to incur the costs of repeating and retraining new workers.

ACTION STEP

Review current and future job openings in your organization and consider why Younger Generations might - or might not - be the best recruits for them.

Recruit Using High Technology Apps and Websites

It has often been noted that younger generations love to use high tech devices and apps. That is true. It is also true that Boomers and members of other age groups often like high technological innovations too. For this reason, using the latest online and app-based recruiting tools is a good idea today, no matter who you are trying to hire.

There is one additional reason, however, to post jobs on platforms like LinkedIn—people who find your jobs using those services will be tech-savvy, as opposed to individuals who find your jobs by looking through your company's job postings, or old-fashioned job ads in newspapers. (Yes, they still exist.) Using high-tech ways to reach applicants is a way to be sure that the applicants who find you and apply will already possess a high level of technical and computer skills.

ACTION STEP

Meet with some of your Younger Generations employees and ask them which tools they would use to look for jobs if they were on the market today.

Offer Training that Supports Job Performance and Advancement

All workers feel reassured when they know they will get the training they need to fulfill the tasks that are a vital part of their jobs. This knowledge goes a long way toward alleviating any insecurities that applicants might feel about things like whether they have the skills they need to perform well, and how they will learn systems that they will need to use.

Contrastingly, for Boomers who are considering job offers, the promise of training can be a big determining factor that convinces them to choose your company.

Some Effective Interview Questions to Ask Younger Applicants

- What is important to you in your life and your work?

- What excites you?

- What frustrated you most in your previous jobs?

- This is what our company stands for. Does it resonate with your values?

- Where do you hope to be in your career in one year, in two years, in five years, and further into the future?

- What kind of personal skills and aptitudes would you like to bring to your job with us?

- Here is a copy of the job description for the position we are hoping to fill. How would you enlarge and expand it to make it more exciting and rewarding? Are there any duties or skills you would like to see us add, or take away?

- How important to you is learning on the job?

- We value and reward teamwork. How important is teamwork to you? Can you describe team experiences you have had in the past?

- We offer great training, including a management and leadership training program. Is this something you would be interested in?

A Final Thought on Jobs that Offer No Advancement

As we close this chapter, this is a good time to mention the fact that some jobs do not promise advancement—yet you still need to fill them. A related consideration is that not every job applicant is looking for a position that promises career growth or a long period of employment.

If you are hiring food servers for a restaurant, for example, the jobs you are offering might, or might not, promise promotions. If you are hiring automotive service writers for a large dealership, the same could be true.

Numerous other positions that attract younger generations fall into that same "no promotions ahead" category. Maybe you are hiring short-term summer employees to park cars at your theme park, or at NASCAR races; or maybe you are hiring brand ambassadors to set up and monitor store displays; perhaps you're looking for young, strong workers to work in your lumber yard or gardening store.

From the other side of the hiring relationship, there are some applicants—no matter their age or demographic group—who are not looking for long-running jobs or advancement. Consider one classic example: an actor who only wants to work in your restaurant until that "big break" comes along.

In cases like these, promising advancement will not do

much to fill your available job (or jobs). You can set aside many of the observations we have made in this chapter and follow a more streamlined and straightforward approach to hiring that centers on recruiting candidates with good employment records, appropriate skills, and a good attitude.

When it comes right down to it, a great attitude could be the most important attribute of any, whether you are hiring young college grads, elders who are seeking jobs to work during their retirement years, or anyone in between.

In Conclusion:

Although many younger generations are looking for jobs today, it is a mistake to assume that the best of them will find their way to the jobs you need filled. It takes some specific skills—those that we have explored in this chapter—to recruit the best candidates from the "Younger Generations" generation.

CHAPTER ELEVEN

Transforming Your Personal and Family Life with Ingaged Leadership

Even though I envisioned this book as one about leadership with a focus on business, people have told me they are applying its lessons in their communities, family activities, and charitable work. I value such a perspective; life affords us many opportunities to lead beyond the sphere of professional life.

was particularly happy that several people suggested that the book's principles of Ingaged Leadership could be applied, in very positive ways, to family life.

How can you use the Ingagement philosophy in your family and in building a healthier work/life balance? This chapter is all about exploring that balance.

The New Secret of Establishing a Healthy Work/Life Balance

Many people today are concerned with establishing a healthier balance between their professional and personal lives. Some are worried simply because they are working too hard and placing greater weight on professional success than they place on living fulfilling personal lives.

Companies are thinking about this issue a lot today—they are even offering seminars and workshops to help their employees. If you read popular magazines, you have seen many articles on the issue.

Yet in general, people are trying to establish a healthy balance in a way that seems flawed to me . . .

They concentrate only on the work aspect of the issue, and not on the personal.

There is some wisdom in this approach. If people are working too hard, or too long, they can find help by reducing the number of hours they work, by giving up some responsibilities on the job, or by delegating more effectively. They can find a new job or change career paths and possibly take up less demanding professions.

Here is a suggestion: What if instead of focusing on the work aspect of the work/life balance, we learned to place more emphasis on the personal side of the equation? What if we concentrated on getting much more from our personal lives by practicing them in ways that are more exciting, more fulfilling, and more Ingaged? What if we became leaders not only in our professional lives, but in our personal lives as well?

By fortifying our personal lives, we can establish a healthy balance without weakening our careers—how strong this can be. How many people do you know today, who *want* to be less successful in their careers? How many people will succeed at maintaining a work/life balance if they know they must become less professionally successful to keep it going?

We live in a world that is filled with success-oriented people. I am one of them, and I expect that you are too; success is nothing to apologize for. The secret of building a healthy balance for people like us means becoming just as accomplished in our personal lives as we are in our careers.

And how can we do that? We can do it by applying the principles of Ingaged Leadership in our personal lives in many of the same ways we apply them in business.

Unlock the Power of Three Things

I would like to explain one very positive approach to Ingagement that I have used in my own family. I call it "Three Things," and I would like to recommend it to you. Here is how it works...

A few years ago, I started to ask everyone at my family's dinner table to describe three positive things that had happened to them during the course of the day. I don't think they understood exactly why I was doing that—I probably didn't grasp the full importance of it either at the time.

At first, my children were a little skeptical, maybe even a little resistant. Their attitude conveyed an unspoken thought, "Oh, Dad . . . why should I have to do this?"

But then they seemed to warm-up to the idea. Even more importantly, they realized that they needed to be on the lookout for good things throughout the day because they knew we would be discussing them at dinner. That expectation created a big change in the way we were all experiencing our days and in the way we were interacting with each other. We were looking for good things, so instead of seeing the world through negative eyeglasses, we began to see it through positive ones.

After all, so many of us have developed the habit of seeing our day in terms of the negatives, so that is what we talk about. We had a bad day at work, the checkout lines were long at the grocery, the train home was delayed, the other drivers were crazy; we miss the positives. But with a simple shift, we can learn to turn around that way of thinking and seeing the world.

ACTION STEP

I would encourage you to experiment with Three Things over the next two months, and to let me know the effect it has on you and those around you.

Shift Your Focus to the Positive

I recommend telling people five positive things for every comment that could possibly be interpreted as negative—so in effect, you are operating on a ratio of 5 to 1 in positive versus ambiguous or less-than-positive communications. This practice will transform your leadership on the job, and it will produce surprising transformations in the way you interact with your family members, friends, and in fact, with everyone around you.

Many of us don't spend enough time giving positive feedback. Some of us say nothing at all until we feel the need to comment or correct something that we think someone is doing wrong. Over time, this negative pattern causes others to feel unappreciated and so defensive that when you approach them, they know that you are unhappy with them. Is that good leadership? Is it a good way to interact with the people you love?

In contrast, you can be on the lookout for good things and call attention to them in positive ways. Concentrate not on perfection, but on the progress and hard work that you see in other people. If you apply this philosophy consistently, everyone around you will be happier, more motivated, and less distracted by worry. Please try it, and again, let me know how it has helped you.

ACTION STEP

Identify three important activities that seem to have you blocked. Try to reframe them in positive, not negative ways and see the difference it makes.

Express Appreciation to People Every Day

Expressing appreciation seems like a small thing to do, but just like using the Three Things, it exerts a surprisingly profound force on everyone around you. You can express appreciation to members of your family, to people who work for the same charities and organizations that you do, and to people you meet everywhere as you go about your life.

If the babysitter you hired to watch your kids one night did an especially caring and capable job, mention how much you appreciate that. Express appreciation for the gas station attendant who washes your windshield; to the waitperson who did an exceptional job attending to your family at a restaurant; to the woman who holds the door of the ATM to make life a little more pleasant for you instead of letting it close in your face.

Every time you express appreciation, you are creating a more positive world, both for you and for everyone around you.

ACTION STEP

Tell someone right now that you appreciate something he or she has done for you. Pick up the phone and make a call to do it if you need to. How did that make you feel? Who is the next person you will appreciate?

Accept the Fact that Other People Often Have Ideas that are as Good as Yours, or Possibly Better

Learn to suspend judgment in interactions with other people by letting go and allowing them to surprise you by doing things the way *they* want to. We have already explored this leadership concept in this book. I am here to tell you it can produce transformational results in the quality of your family and personal life.

Here is a small experiment for you to try: If you have a child, try to see everything you say and do through his or her eyes. Your son just came to you with a suggestion for a summer program he would like to participate in, for example, or your daughter wants to go on vacation with her best friend's family. If you were your son or daughter and expressed desires like these, how would you feel if your idea gets summarily shot down by Mom or Dad?

Accept the idea that the people around you are just as smart as you are, and sometimes smarter. You are not the person who gives definite permission for everything. Do bear in mind, of course, that part of being an effective parent sometimes means denying permission for certain things. Does your daughter want to go swimming with sharks, for example, or travel to a dangerous part of the world? Does your son suddenly announce that he wants to drop out of college a few months before he is due to graduate? Remember that you don't have to approve *everything*. As in your professional life, it is a matter of exercising positive leadership. But before you deny permission, take a little time to ask, "Why?" so you can determine what the real issues are. Then, facilitate decision-making in a positive and Ingaged way.

ACTION STEP

Think about the people around you in your family and personal contexts. Are you empowering them or limiting them? Consider how you can do better.

Practice Ingaged Listening

You unlock the power of Ingaged listening when you learn to stop listening for things other people say that you think are wrong...and start listening for the things that are right. In doing so, you build people up, encourage their positive feelings of self-worth about themselves, and receive a much larger percentage of the ideas and information that they are sending your way.

Following up with exploratory, deeper questions is another important part of Ingaged listening. You will know you are approaching this positive ability when you hear yourself making statements like, "Can we explore that idea of yours more, so I can better understand your thought process?" or, "I never thought of that before. Can you help me understand?"

ACTION STEP

In the next three conversations you have, step mentally back and consider how well you are listening. Have you heard something from that other person that seems promising, positive, or maybe even brilliant? What does that tell you about the listening habits you have developed?

Value and Practice Curiosity and Learning

Companies function on a higher level by becoming In-gaged learning organizations, and families, friendships and organizations can do the same thing. When they do, everyone becomes happier and more invested in living life to the fullest.

How can you cultivate a spirit of learning all around you in your personal life? One thing I have learned is that you cannot delegate a thirst and joy for learning. You must lead by example, which means becoming a curious person; someone who has a genuine love of knowledge about the world around you. Curiosity is the leadership force that turns underperforming organizations into stars, and it can transform everything about your personal life.

Curiosity is the force that gets you involved in the world. What is new in your family, in your community, in everything you encounter in the world? When you develop an enthusiasm to learn and know, you improve the quality of life for yourself, and for everyone around you.

ACTION STEP

Make a list of four or five things that really appeal to you that you have not taken the time to explore or enjoy. Pick one or two and get going.

Practice Ingaged Leadership in Your Community Organizations

The point of assuming leadership positions in your community and in your personal life is not to gain respect, or even to build connections that can help you professionally. It is to make your community, and the world, a better place.

So, what is the best way to become a leader in your religious community, in the charities you are a part of, among the other parents at your children's school, or in the gated community in which you live? Applying the same principles of Ingaged Leadership that you have learned in this book is the way to go. You will get ahead without trying to get ahead, and you will become a leader by trying to do good for others.

Applied in these ways, Ingaged Leadership has the power to establish the kind of fruitful work/life balance that might have otherwise been just out of your reach in the past. You

ACTION STEP

If you are already involved in groups, stop to think about the style of leadership and interaction you have been using in them. Make a list of specific ways that you could apply more Ingaged Leadership in them - and be ready to be positively surprised.

will enjoy a much more fulfilling family and personal life and make a meaningful difference in the world.

In Summary:

Ingaged Leadership can become Ingaged living. I invite you to discover its power to transform your life.

Conclusion

You have explored many concepts throughout this book, and it is my hope that you are excited about what you have read. You have discovered what Ingaged Leadership is, why it is effective, and how to use it. You have also discovered action steps along the way to help you put Ingaged Leadership into daily practice.

But where should you begin? Start with areas that you have identified as "areas of opportunity" as you have read each page—concepts that made you think, "This is an area that could produce some excellent results for me if I address it now."

I would suggest that it would be best to start with two or three ideas, write them down, commit to acting on them, create a plan for each, and execute them to the best of your ability.

Bringing other people into that process is very important. Approach them and simply state, "I just read this book and I feel that we should now do these things."

When you bring other people into the process, you greatly increase the likelihood that the changes you want to make will actually happen—this is almost always the case.

An example from my personal life illustrates the point. I am a man of variable weight and every now and then, I need to go on a diet. When I tell people that I am going on a diet, I find myself successful. Alternatively, when I go on what I call "secret diets" and tell myself, "I am just going to do it on my own," the meal comes and I end up saying, "I'll start tomorrow." Then, "tomorrow" comes and I say, "I'll start tomorrow," once again. But sharing my plans brings me the success I desire.

If you pick a few ideas from this book and commit to implementing them, and share that commitment with your people, change will happen.

After you have successfully accomplished the first two or three things that you committed to, pick up the book again and choose two or three more key things you would like to work on, and implement them.

Supporting Research

If I were you, after reading this book I would likely be thinking, "It is great that Evan believes so strongly in Ingagement and that he feels so positive about it, but where's the proof that it actually works?"

hat is a good question to ask, and it is one that I have asked myself. I would like to address it in two ways: First, I will provide some statistics from studies that have established the effectiveness of Ingagement. Second, I will offer case studies that illustrate how Ingagement has produced superlative results.

Research: Gallup Study Shows that Engagement Builds Highly Competitive Companies

Gallup Consulting's "Employee Engagement: What's Your Engagement Ratio" is a landmark study on the benefits of employee engagement within organizations. The study's findings emerged from more than 30 years of research involving more than 17 million employees.

To quote from that study:

"The world's top-performing organizations understand that employee engagement is a force that drives business outcomes. Research shows that engaged employees are more productive employees. They are more profitable, more customer-focused, safer, and more likely to withstand temptations to leave the organization. In the best organizations, employee engagement transcends a human resources initiative—it is the way they do business. Employee engagement is a strategic approach supported by tactics for driving improvement and organizational change. The best performing companies know that developing an employee engagement strategy and linking it to the achievement of corporate goals will help them win in the marketplace."

Gallup created a "macro-level indicator," called the Engagement Ratio, that serves as a benchmark for the level of employee engagement within organizations. It is a numerical ratio that compares the level of engaged employees to those who are actively disengaged.

Gallup determined that ratio by asking employees at different companies to respond to the following statements and rate which were true, and which were not:

- "I know what is expected of me at work."

- "I have the materials and equipment I need to do my work to the best of my ability."

- "At work, I have the opportunity to do what I do best every day."

- "In the last seven days, I have received recognition or praise for doing good work."

- "My supervisor, or someone at work, seems to care about me as a person."

- "There is someone at work who encourages my development."

- "At work, my opinions seem to count."

- "The mission or purpose of my organization makes me feel like my job is important."

- "My associates or fellow employees are committed to doing quality work."

- "I have a best friend at work."

- "In the last six months, someone at work has talked to me about my progress."

- "This last year, I have had opportunities at work to learn and grow."

Based on the responses to these questions, Gallup determined the level of employee engagement in the companies involved in the study and found that in average-performing organizations, only 33% of employees were engaged, 49% were not engaged, and 18% were actively disengaged. This represents an engagement ratio of 1.83:1, or the ratio of engaged employees to disengaged.

Gallup also determined that in world-class, highly competitive organizations, an average of 67% of employees were engaged; 26% of employees were not engaged; and only 7% were actively disengaged. This represents an engagement ratio of 9.57:1, or the ratio of engaged employees to disengaged.

Gallup concluded that "world-class organizations . . . have an engagement ratio of more than 9:1." Gallup then went on to make some extraordinary conclusions about the performance of world-class companies (those in the top quartile on its Employee Engagement ratio) when compared to companies that fall in the bottom quartile:

- Companies with world-class engagement achieve 3.9 times the earnings per share (EPS) growth.

- Companies with world-class engagement exhibit a "dramatic difference" in improved absenteeism, employee retention, workplace safety, customer satisfaction, productivity, and profitability.

Further Research: Data Shows that Ingagement Builds Profits

In a landmark study conducted by *Franchise Business Review*, 24,050 franchisees representing more than 300 companies were surveyed over a one-year period. One goal was to try to establish a correlation between Ingaged communication and organizational success, while another goal was to uncover and understand the key factors that lead to organizational Ingagement.

The study employed an analytical tool called the "Ingage Barometer," which was developed jointly by my company Ingage Consulting and a research organization called Liminality Inc.

The Ingage Barometer is a sophisticated tool that evaluates levels of Ingagement by asking a battery of questions to everyone within an organization. Based on analysis of those responses, organizations are grouped into quartiles. The top quartile encompasses companies that engage in the most inclusive communication, and as you might expect, the companies in the bottom quartile do not.

The results of this study of franchisees concluded that in Ingaged organizations:

- Those in the top quartile were 3.7 times more likely to report strong financial results than organizations in the bottom quartile.

- Those in the top quartile did much more to promote the success of their brand. In fact, not one of the more than 6000 Ingaged organizations in the top quartile stated that they would not recommend their franchise and its system. What about franchisees in the bottom quartile? 47% of them stated that they *would not* actively recommend their franchise to potential new franchisees.

The willingness of franchisees to advocate for their companies is critical for a very simple reason. When individuals are thinking of buying a franchise, the first thing they do is call current owners to ask some critical questions about the franchise. Does the parent company communicate effectively with franchise owners? Does it go the extra mile to provide support when and where support is needed?

As you can see, the evidence is quite dramatic that Ingagement fuels the success and growth of organizations.

Acknowledgements

I want to acknowledge and graciously so many people for the roles they have played in my life and in the creation of this book. Without their knowledge, support, and inspiration, I would never have become the person I am today, and I would certainly never have undertaken putting my thoughts down on paper.

First, I want to thank my wife Laura for her love and support of our entire family. A true life-partner, she shares my eagerness to learn to be a better leader. Laura has been with me at seminars at the Center for Authentic Leadership and elsewhere, discussing concepts with me at all hours and helping to deepen my understanding of leadership. She is a remarkably successful businesswoman as well. She joined Cambridge Technology Partners early in her career when it was a relatively small, $9 million company. During her tenure, it grew to a billion-dollar company, with a lot of the credit going to her work there in many roles, including Senior VP for Human Resources. I have never known anyone who can equal her ability to create a safe and caring space where people can interact. She has built success on success, thanks in part to her empathy for others at every stage. She is now owner of Artful Healings, an inspiring company that helps people gain health through traditional healing arts. I know that many adventures lie ahead for us.

I want to give special thanks to my mother Sonya, and Paul my late father, who passed away at the time when I was completing this book. My father was a unique man, the former owner of a small business that he ran with vision, passion, and the highest of standards. He was widely respected, the kind of man for whom people would do anything. When I was only 10 years old, he let me start to work in the family business, and from that age I began to learn how to manage a business. (How many people are privileged to have that kind of experience from such an early age?) My mother is just as remarkable, a woman of incredible strength and conviction of opinion. Without her devotion to me, I would probably never have graduated from high school, let alone college. When I needed someone to step up and advocate for me, she was always there and never let me down.

Special thanks go to my very different, very wonderful children Aaron, Alex and Alton. I expect that it has not always been completely easy for them to have a dad who has been so busy working, traveling, and claiming time to take part in a committed study of leadership. My thanks and love go to them every day.

Thanks go equally to my sisters Shira and Nina, and to

my brother John; they have all been such a great part of my life. As a businesswoman, Nina was been nothing short of an inspiration, entering the business world as a technology saleswoman at a time when the field was almost completely dominated by men. And John and Shira have contributed so much to my life, in so many ways.

I offer profound appreciation and thanks to Alan Green-burg and Howard Brodsky, the co-CEOs of CCA Global Partners. I started working there in 1988 when the company was called Carpet Co-op of America; I was only the fifth em-ployee on the payroll. These two men placed their trust in me completely and gave me the opportunity to learn and grow. They let me start a marketing department, introduce a training division, and launch a variety of new enterprises that included an international design group, new franchise operations, and new initiatives that included a co-op that issues $65 billion in mortgages, and even a formalwear company. During my 20 years at CCA, we achieved an average annual growth rate of 29% compounded. By the time I left the company, I had achieved $5 billion in system-wide sales and was responsible for 70% of the firm's overall profitability. I accomplished a lot, but none of it would have been possible without the vision and support of these two men who are like brothers to me.

I want to acknowledge Jan Smith, the inspiring leader who founded the Center for Authentic Leadership in 1985. The Future Thinking and Leadership Intensive programs that she created led me to discover new vistas of Ingaged and visionary leadership. The three levels of communication that I write about in this book are based in part on the Communication Meter that she created, and I thank her for that.

I offer great thanks to the remarkable people at both Ingage Consulting and Tortal Consultants. I have learned so much from all of you and have often been inspired by your insights and tireless work. I wish to offer special thanks to Deb Binder (a woman who is so wonderful that I have hired her on three different occasions) and Cordell Riley, who brings unequalled insight into the world of franchising in the automotive sector. Great thanks also go to all members of the Ingage and Tortal team, including Janet Brideaux, Stephanie Stiles, Mike Ziglar, Joshua R. De La Vega, Matthew Cole, Brannon Dreher, Erin Brennan, Adria Myers, Desiree Lackey, Lee Wedgeworth and Gregg Dumont.

Thanks also go to Ellen Liberman, a brilliant and incisive editor who reviewed this manuscript before publication and offered many helpful ideas. Her comments and suggestions made this book more readable, more insightful, and much more positive in tone.

Finally, I want to thank Barry Lenson, the editor and business journalist who helped me organize my ideas and put them together into this book. He listened and talked to me for many hours. Along the way, we laughed, exchanged opinions and ideas, and enjoyed one of the more productive collaborations that I can recall.

About the Author

Evan Hackel has helped start over 20 businesses, turned around a bankrupt $700 million franchise business and grown it to $2 Billion in four years. He was part of the team that grew CCA Global Partners to $10 billion in system-wide sales in 20 years. Evan is considered an expert in Franchising, Cooperatives, business startups and general management. He is CEO of Tortal Training, a leading training development company, and Principal and Founder of Ingage Consulting. Evan is the host of Training Unleashed and author of Ingaging Leadership. Evan speaks on Seeking Excellence, Better Together, Ingaging Leadership and Attitude is Everything. To engage Evan as a speaker, visit www.evanspeaksfranchising.com. Follow @ehackel

About Ingage
Consulting

Ingage Consulting, headquartered in Woburn, Massachusetts, is the foremost provider of specialized management consulting services for leaders of franchises, cooperatives, buying groups and dealer networks. Drawing directly from his leadership experience at several business cooperatives and group organizations, Founder and Principal Evan Hackel works to make his client organizations more successful from the inside out by bolstering organizational Ingagement, empowerment, and collaboration.

We are life-long learners and are committed to constantly evolving and getting better at what we do.

We believe our organization needs to exemplify everything we help our customers achieve. As such, we hire people who share our values and strategic direction and offer them a great place to work.

We publish and openly share best practices. We are educators, not just consultants.

We grow our business organically, through acquisition and by aligning with like-minded companies.

Ingage Consulting
400 Trade Center
Suite 5900
Woburn MA 01801-7472
TEL: (781) 281-9390

About Tortal Training

Tortal Training, headquartered in Charlotte, North Carolina, is a full-service training and development firm that specializes in developing interactive eLearning solutions. Tortal Training is the only training service partner that uses strategic Ingagement methodologies. This helps organizations with distributed workforces leverage their talent development to maximize training effectiveness and drive sustainable business results.

Customers choose Tortal Training over the competition to get training that works. By tying increased Ingagement to all products and services, Tortal Training sets itself apart from DIY options, LMS companies, and even internal capabilities through customer education and demonstrated effectiveness.

Tortal also offers online training solutions, speakers' services, and a range of additional services in the training sector. Tortal Training has achieved remarkable success for clients from a number of industries that include advanced manufacturing, automotive, commercial cleaning, emergency cleaning, healthcare, hair salons, food service, home organization, painting, personal fitness and gyms, property damage remediation, rent-to-own, and retail.

We value collaboration and believe the strongest teams share information and jump in with both feet.

We value honesty and know that listening is a critical component of openness.

We will build trust and lasting relationships only by being our authentic selves.

We are open to trying new things, open to new ideas, and just as open to receiving feedback as we are to giving it.

Tortal Training
14825 Ballantyne Village Way
Building A, Suite 240-4
Charlotte, NC 28277
TEL: (704) 323-8953

Index

Index

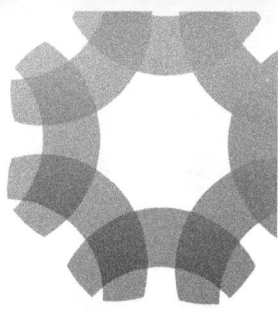

About Ingaging Leadership:

Ingagement is a philosophy for leaders who believe that it is not enough to tell people what to do, but to Ingage their minds, creativity and even their emotions and their hearts.

Ingaged Leadership starts with a belief that when you align people and create an organization where everyone works together in partnership, that organization becomes vastly more successful.

As you will discover in *Ingaging Leadership,* Ingagement isn't a single action that you take just once. It is an ongoing, dynamic business practice that has the power to transform your organization, your people, you, and ultimately, your success.

A Free Study Guide Is Now Available

Some readers have told me that they have begun to use *Ingaging Leadership* as a tool to build teams at work. Others have told me that they are discussing the book in book groups, professional organizations and in groups that meet in their companies. In response, we have just published a special Book Discussion Guide that serves as a companion to the main volume. You can download a copy of it for free on the Ingage Consulting website at Ingage.net.

Please Tell Me More

I am hoping that you and I can grow together as leaders, so I invite you to send further comments and suggestions to me at ehackel@Ingage.net.

CPSIA information can be obtained
at www.ICGtesting.com
Printed in the USA
BVHW042108270720
584825BV00014B/395

9 781628 657241